A simple yet comprehensive gu
childbirth and

Having a Baby Easily

a guide to natural birth

by

MARGARET Y. BRADY M.Sc.

THORSONS PUBLISHERS LIMITED
Wellingborough, Northamptonshire

First paperback edition (completely revised and reset) May 1981
Second Impression November 1981
Third Impression April 1983

British Library Cataloguing in Publication Data

Brady, Margaret Y
   Having a baby easily. — Revised ed.
   1. Pregnancy
   2. Childbirth
   I. Title
   612.6'3   RG525

   ISBN 0-7225-0668-6

Printed and bound in Great Britain

Contents

Acknowledgements

I would like to thank Dr Monica Latto very much for kindly reading the script for me, and Mrs Sally Rose for her most helpful comments, and also other members of the National Childbirth Trust for their interest.

I would also especially like to thank Dr Douglas Latto for so kindly writing such an appreciative Foreword to this new edition.

Dedication

To the thousands of mothers who, over the years, have written to me for advice and help about their babies.

Foreword

It is a great happiness to me and a privilege to write this preface for Margaret Brady's *Having a Baby Easily*.

Margaret Brady is an enthusiastic student and advanced thinker on health and nutrition. She has been intensely interested in natural childbirth ever since her first baby was born, and her interest continues today now she has great grand-children.

I myself have been interested in the field for many years and have been concerned with it professionally. I am, therefore, grateful to the author for sharing her wide experience and views on this important subject. She has, I believe, the insight and imagination to ask the right questions, and the honesty in pursuit of the answers to be true to the facts as she finds them. In addition she has included the importance of nutrition in pregnancy, has made a great study of it and has lectured on the making of wholemeal bread and allied subjects in many parts of this country.

Margaret Brady removes the fear of childbirth by a simple explanation to the mother of the whole process; this knowledge automatically allays fear. Like myself, she likes the father to be present at the birth as the baby belongs especially to both parents; and this sharing of the birth brings the whole family unit closer together. It takes away fear of subsequent pregnancies and enhances the mother's whole obstetric future.

This work by Margaret Brady will be found to be of great value both to the practitioner, and to the expectant mother. I wish the book a wide readership. It deserves it.

DOUGLAS LATTO
M.B., Ch.B., D.Obst., RCOG, MRCOG

The beginning, as you know, is always the most important part, especially in dealing with anything young and tender.

Plato

Introduction

I am deeply grateful to the very many mothers who, over the years, have written to me to thank me for my book *Having a Baby Easily*, and to tell me of the help that it has been to them.

My aim was, and still is, to help mothers to create babies who are mentally and physically healthy, to try to ensure that birth is the natural function it ought to be, free from undue pain, to bring down our distressingly high infant mortality rate and to foster breast-feeding. Though there has been much new work in these fields in the last forty years, including the considerable growth in medical technology, there is still a long way to go before the above aims are fully achieved.

It is my conviction that mothers themselves hold the key to easy natural births, and it is the object of this book to help them to find and use this key. It is not my intention to lay down hard-and-fast rules, but to present mothers with ideas about what they themselves can do, and to adapt these ideas if necessary to their own specific needs.

MARGARET BRADY
Cookham 1981

1.

Going About It in the Right Way: Three Fundamentals

The birth of a baby means complete physical fulfilment of a woman's most fundamental function of reproduction and motherhood, but more than this it is also a big step along her road to emotional and spiritual fulfilment too. Having a baby should be a wonderful experience full of joy and deep happiness, and one that opens the door to endless new schemes and interests. It is a perfectly natural process and pregnancy should be an exceptionally happy and healthy time. Severe pain, impaired health let alone death of either mother or baby cannot be part of God's plan, and so we should be able to learn how to avoid such things.

To create a new human being is a great privilege and a great responsibility, so young mothers naturally want to know how to do the job well.

A Unique Opportunity
In pregnancy expectant mothers have a unique opportunity. No-one else can do what they can do to promote easy natural childbirth and to create babies with healthy minds and bodies, and the aim of this book is to help mothers to achieve these ends.

Having a baby is a threefold function. It is:

1. Creative
2. Athletic
3. Spiritual

All three should work together as a team. Neglect of any one of them may be at the root of possible troubles during the pregnancy, or at the birth, or even with the baby after it is born.

Since having a baby is a creative function, the mother needs to have the best possible raw materials for the job. Since it is also an athletic function, she needs some athletic training, and since it is also a spiritual function, she needs to cultivate the right spiritual and emotional approach.

These are the three fundamentals on which having a perfect and healthy baby can be based, and any healthy woman need not fear motherhood if she will remember these things and act on them. She will then have every chance of finding the birth both thrilling and interesting, even if she does not quite reach the goal of finding it painless.

It is, of course, also very desirable for both parents to be in good health themselves, preferably even before conception takes place. The importance of the good health of the father, as well as of the mother, is well recognized by people dealing with farm stock and race horses, but unfortunately is rarely considered to be important in human beings.

Raw Materials

The essential raw materials for creating a new baby are the FOOD, WATER, AIR and SUNSHINE the mother receives. *In no other field of creative human endeavour is the matter of the best possible raw materials needed for the job in hand more vitally important than it is with expectant mothers.*

Having the best possible raw materials not only involves the positive aspect of supplying the right ones, but it must include the more negative aspect of avoiding the wrong kinds of foods. Anyone who deals with growing things, such as farmers, poultry keepers or gardeners all know that though they must start with good stock, their stock must also have the right kind of high quality food for its growth if they are to be successful in their work.

The usual advice to expectant mothers is that they should have a good mixed diet, including plenty of fruit and vegetables, and that dairy produce is good for them. This is alright as far as it goes, but it is not enough. *The need for real 100 per cent wholewheat bread in place of white bread and less white sugar needs to be very strongly stressed.* Actually, some mothers may, regrettably, make few real changes in their eating habits, and may continue to live largely on over-refined and over-processed foods as they and their friends have done all their lives. Unfortunately, this too often means having modern 'technological' foods which are often of too poor nutritional quality to be suitable for expectant mothers.

Need for Positive Creative Action

According to World Health Organization statistics, the Infant Mortality rate for England and Wales is notably higher than that of many other countries, such as Sweden, the Netherlands and Japan, though lower than that of the United States. Too many babies are born prematurely, underweight or handicapped, and wonderful work is done by devoted and skilful doctors and nurses to care for such babies. It is here that expectant mothers can do a great deal to help themselves. The mother's food and general habits are vitally important and the mother can start improving her ante-natal preparations by supplying herself with high quality food, and by taking adequate exercise and adequate rest and relaxation.

Athletic Training

Just as the right raw materials are essential for any creative job, so is the right kind of athletic training essential for any athletic feat. Just as athletes go 'into training' for their athletic events, so also do expectant mothers need to go into training for the athletic event of giving birth. Their muscles, like those of other athletes, need to be strengthened for their coming job, and their breathing needs to be trained.

In no other function of human athletic effort is the matter of suitable athletic training for the job in hand more important than it is for the athletic function of birth. (See Chapter 5).

Spiritual Function

The third essential, the spiritual side of having a baby has not always been given its due importance as an integral part of having a baby. This function refers to the whole mental, emotional and spiritual outlook of the mother. To be aware that one is taking part in the great creative forces of life is a wonderful realization, and there can be a deep spiritual significance in pregnancy.

Easy Births

In some places, among more primitive peoples who live on simple foods and follow a simple, energetic, outdoor life without any fears of motherhood, babies are still born quickly and easily. This should be our objective too. We owe it to our babies to try to ensure for them as quick and easy and natural an entry into the world as possible.

It is in carrying out sensible ante-natal preparations that mothers can confidently develop their inherent natural ability to create beautiful and healthy babies and to give birth with joy and without severe pain. This is a serious objective, not a pipe dream.

Making a really good job of having a baby can give great satisfaction, and it is encouraging for the mother when she knows that during the nine months of waiting she is actively working to create a healthy and beautiful little baby, as well as making beautiful little garments in which to dress her baby when he comes.

The young mother-to-be should be able to carry out the suggestions given here, while at the same time living a normal and happy life.

The Baby

The work and care that a mother puts into producing a loved and healthy baby is of great value in itself. Each baby is entitled to be accepted and loved for what he is, and no parents should, by applying theories or statistics to their child, feel that, in some way, his differences or even shortcomings are due to the mother's failure in her appointed task. There is still a great deal to learn about pregnancy and birth, and sometimes there may be unknown factors, such as heredity, or even environmental pollution which, on rare occasions, might interfere with the best ante-natal preparations.

Real deformities are fortunately very rare, but when such

potentially tragic births do occur, the family may be able subsequently to achieve heights of love and unity by accepting such children, so that they transcend the potential disaster that has so wantonly arrived in the family unit.

If, in spite of all a mother's ante-natal preparations, the birth should, for some unknown reason, prove to be a difficult one, the mother should not blame herself. Indeed, she can console herself that she has done her best and that her diet and exercises will have helped to make her baby strong and healthy, even if they did not make the birth easy.

Drugs and Tranquillizers

Every individual tends to react differently to drugs, and even those which are accepted as 'safe' may be bad for a developing embryo, as they may cross the placenta. So, unless specifically prescribed by a doctor, drugs should be avoided. Fortunately, many of the conditions for which drugs tend to be taken may well be eliminated if the diet and other suggestions given here are carried out. If minor disabilities do emerge, then natural methods, such as missing a meal or having a warm bath followed by a warm fruit or vegetable broth drink or herbal tea in bed, may be all that is needed. Natural food supplements are not drugs.

Thalidomide

A warning of the damage that drugs can do to the foetus in the early months was most tragically given to mothers by the drug thalidomide. This drug was repeatedly claimed to be absolutely safe, yet hundreds of babies were born physically deformed through their mothers having taken thalidomide, often under medical advice, in the early months of their pregnancy.

Natural Childbirth

Increasing numbers of mothers now prepare themselves in advance for their baby's birth and are now well aware of what their own part in the birth will be. They can anticipate that the birth will mean quite hard work, analogous to mountaineering, but that the pain will not be too severe or prolonged.

The mother should be able to have her husband with her for the birth. Indeed, where the father has taken part in the birth, both mother and father have found it a most memorable experience. Some doctors and midwives are very interested in natural childbirth, and their understanding and co-operation are invaluable for its successful functioning.

'Foresight'

'Foresight' is an 'Association for the Promotion of Pre-Conceptual Care'. It teaches that, to help parents to have perfect babies, both parents should work to get themselves into the best possible health *before* conception takes place, and also that the mother's diet during her pregnancy must be of the highest nutritional quality. (See *Useful Addresses*.)

The National Childbirth Trust

There is now a splendid organization, the National Childbirth Trust (see *Useful Addresses*), which aims to help in education for parenthood. They hold classes and seminars in many areas of the country, with instruction in exercises, relaxation, and trained and controlled breathing to facilitate the birth. The Trust will supply the names and addresses of their branches, groups and the counsellors who will advise and train expectant mothers, talking over ante-natal problems, and also giving post-natal support. The N.C.T. counsellors also give advice and encouragement over breast-feeding, so all expectant mothers would do well to contact the Trust to find their local representative. They also supply leaflets and cassettes for those mothers unable to find a class near enough.

Rewards of the Job

Parenthood means hard work and long hours. It is a job which demands self-control, lots of love, ingenuity, and lots of patience, but it is also a job which, more than most, brings the most wonderful rewards, bringing joy and happiness to the parents, as well as health and happiness to the children. There can hardly be a more worthwhile job than that of giving the rising generation a really good start in life with health and happiness in childhood. Parenthood is essentially a joint concern, in which both parents unite in creating a happy family by loving and training their children together. Happy families are a great asset to the community.

2.

First Fundamental:
Essential Raw Materials

Food and Food Technology

We all know that our food can affect our health, but many people do not realize just how much modern food technology can damage the nutritional quality of our food. The chemical, physical and biological manipulation of our food has reached amazing proportions. The processed food industry is concerned with making products that taste nice, are attractive to look at, profitable, may have a long shelf-life, and are not immediately harmful; but the technologists generally are not specifically concerned with their products' nutritional values. Such foods are well advertised, and are often very popular, but may be of relatively poor nutritional quality.

Nutritionists have frequently shown that many modern foods are far from nutritionally desirable. The great nutritionist Sir Robert McCarrison studied the matter of food and health very extensively.

Sir Robert, working in India, noted the very different standards of health between different tribes, and he carried out exhaustive feeding tests with different groups of rats, copying the various diets. He found that his rats repeated the health and physical states of the tribes whose food they were having. He also fed one group on what he called a 'poor British diet' (of about 1928) consisting of white bread, lots of sweet tea, cheap tinned meat and cheap tinned jam, with overcooked vegetables, little, if any, fruit and little milk. These rats developed all the diseases of similarly fed humans: they had difficulty in giving birth and in producing healthy young, with the consequent high mortality rates; they also developed behaviour problems, unlike the rats fed on the whole natural diet of the Indian Sikhs.

Sir Robert came to the conclusion that, 'The greatest single factor in the acquisition and maintenance of good health is perfectly constituted food' and his definition of such food was that it should be whole, fresh and with a good proportion eaten raw, and grown on healthy soil. By 'whole' foods is meant foods that have not had valuable nutritional parts needlessly removed, nor have had non-nutritious chemicals added to them. No-one has ever refuted the views of Sir Robert's, but neither has it been officially endorsed. Expectant mothers would be very wise to adopt his teaching as the basis for their own meals, in order to give their babies the best possible start in life, and to help to promote easy natural births.

Nutritional Quality

The general diet of today cannot be said to be 'perfectly constituted' food since it consists too much of the refined, processed, over-cooked, preserved and devitalized foods. Many valuable and natural mineral salts and vitamins are known to be lost in the processes of preserving and manufacture, and the loss of these elements, which are essential for good health, must contribute to the vast incidence of illnesses and degenerative diseases which affect civilized communities today. Living on a normal modern diet, the body's physical hunger may easily be satisfied with the processed foods eaten *before* its fundamental physiological needs for mineral salts and vitamins have been met. Expectant mothers are starting on a period of special physiological activity, with its corresponding needs of just those elements which the modern diet carries in short supply, hence the need for them to choose foods of high natural nutritional quality.

Foods to Select

The advantage of eating foods 'whole' is that the maximum amount of all the nutrients are present, and their natural balance and proportion is retained. If an apple is peeled, instead of being eaten with the skin on – provided that this does not produce any indigestion – one loses not only the roughage value of the skin, but also some of the nutrients that may be concentrated just below the skin, such as iron, phosphorus magnesium and silicon. Similarly, when potatoes are cooked in their skins, it helps to conserve the nutrients in the potatoes. One of the best ways to cook potatoes is to bake them in their skins, when the skins may be eaten with advantage if there is no sickness or indigestion.

Wholewheat Bread

Choosing wholefoods means choosing 100 per cent wholewheat bread in place of white bread, and doing this is one of the most valuable steps expectant mothers can take. To make white flour, the outer coats of the wheat grain, and the growing point, or germ, of the wheat are removed, and just the very white centre part, the endosperm, is used to make white flour. This is then used to make white bread.

However, these outer coats and the wheatgerm contain a great deal of the most valuable and nutritious parts of the wheat, including a little good protein, a large amount of many of the parts of the B vitamin complex (B_1, nicotinic acid, riboflavin, pantothenic acid, pyridoxine, folic acid and biotin) and much of the mineral salts of the grain, (calcium, potassium, phosphorus, iron, copper, magnesium and manganese) nearly all the vitamin E (very important for expectant mothers), and all the bran which is an invaluable source of fibre, and an aid to avoiding constipation.

If one cannot buy 100 per cent wholewheat bread, it is quite simple and also rewarding to make one's own, choosing if possible, organically grown flour.

White flour also has to have four nutrients added to it by law: powdered chalk, now said to be for calcium, but originally added to the national bread as a neutralizing agent *not* as a nutrient; an iron compound; and two B vitamins, B_1 and nicotinic acid – but these are synthetic substitutes for the natural ones. These four additions do not even begin to make good all the nutrients that are lost in making white flour. In addition to the compulsory additives, other additives such as bleaching agents, and anti-staling agents may also be added, if desired by the baker, but such additions do not add to the nutritional quality of bread.

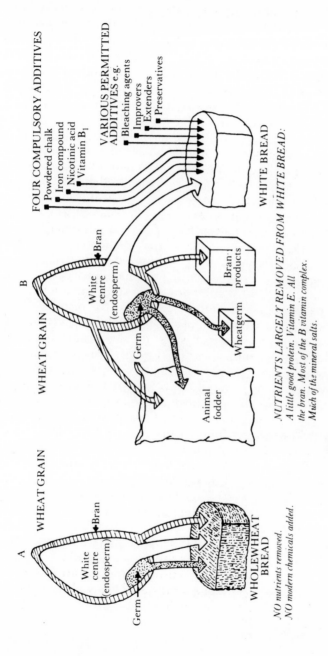

Figure 1. Diagram showing differences between (A) 100 per cent wholewheat bread and (B) white bread.

The diagram on page 23 illustrates the nutritional differences between wholewheat bread and white bread. The parts removed are used to feed farm animals and race horses, though a small amount of them is packeted up and sold as rather expensive food supplements for human consumption. When we see packets of bran and wheatgerm on shop shelves, we should realize that they are there because they have been taken out of someone else's white bread.

In view of the skill, hard work and energy, together with the nutrients of the soil, sun, air and water, that go into growing and harvesting this marvellous food, wheat, it does seem a great tragedy that such a large proportion of the health-giving nutrients of the wheat never reach expectant mothers and their growing babies at all. Yet these are the people for whom these nutrients are particularly important. It would seem possible that years of living on nutritionally inferior white bread is a factor in producing our high infant mortality rate. Too many mothers continue to eat white bread today.

Honey and Molasses
Similarly, white sugar is a deficiency food, having had the vitamins and mineral salts of the sugar cane or sugar beet removed because they are coloured, and also might lead to fermentation when stored. Just the pure, highly concentrated sucrose is crystallized out as white sugar. Expectant mothers are wisest to use a little honey or molasses, instead of white sugar, and to take sugar in its natural form as ripe fruits rather than to eat the refined white sugar.

Ripe Raw Fruit
Raw fruit is most valuable for expectant mothers, particularly oranges, taken daily during pregnancy.

Vegetables and Raw Salads
Vegetables are also a most valuable part of the mother's meals, and when cooked it should be in a minimum of water, for the shortest possible time, with the skins kept on when possible. They tend to make the system alkaline and should be cooked without soda and with only the minimum of salt, and

good servings of two or more should be included daily. Raw vegetable salads are also extremely valuable, but if, as sometimes may happen in the early months, a mother feels that she cannot take raw salads, then freshly-pressed, raw vegetable juices are useful, with extra, cooked vegetables. Raw carrot juice is easy to make (see recipes) and makes a good pre-supper 'cocktail'. Apple muesli makes a good raw food for breakfast (see recipes).

Dairy Produce

Milk, eggs, cheese and butter and yogurt are good foods and are usually well tolerated in pregnancy; but the mother should not force herself to take more than she wants. Milk, cheese and yogurt are particularly valuable sources of calcium. Cheese can be served grated with vegetables or baked potatoes or with vegetable soup. Eggs are a good source of protein and mineral salts. Mothers who cannot take milk may find that they can more readily accept yogurt, or even a good plant milk, such as Plamil.

Good Protein

Adequate, but not excessive amounts of good protein, the food for building the tissues, is needed, but meat is not essential for this purpose, and some mothers may be better without it. If eaten it should only be in small amounts. Apart from dairy produce, excellent protein is supplied by pulse foods including soya products, and nuts, as well as some from the wholewheat bread. Fish is also a useful protein food.

Organically Grown Foods

In the last forty years there has been an enormous increase in the amount of soluble chemical fertilizers used in the growing of our food, and this has been accompanied by a large growth in the amount of poisonous insecticides and pesticides used on the crops. Interesting work has been done, originally by the Soil Association (see *Useful Addresses*), which suggests that crops grown with natural organic manures are better for our health than are those grown with soluble chemical fertilizers. If expectant mothers can obtain organically grown foods –

that is, grown without soluble chemical fertilizers and poisonous sprays – they would be wise to use them. Many factory farming methods would appear to be undesirable, and free-range eggs are preferable to battery-produced eggs.

Suggested Menu for Expectant Mothers

On Waking:
   Drink of diluted unsweetened apple or grape juice or a herb tea, or Vichy water.

Breakfast:
   Drink of pure fresh orange juice. Muesli (see recipe) with a chopped-up eating apple and a dessertspoonful of raisins, or a few prunes, or any fresh raw fruit and milk or yogurt, and 1-2 dessertspoonsful unprocessed wheatgerm, and a little unprocessed bran if there is any tendency to constipation.
   Wholewheat bread (or toast) with butter and honey or black treacle or Marmite. Milk drink.

Mid-morning:
   Drinks as already suggested or clear vegetable broth with Barmene or half-and-half with milk. Or, 1 teaspoonful lemon juice with 1-2 teaspoonsful of honey in hot or cold water, or honey tea, or brose, or raspberry leaf tea.

Lunch:
   1-2 fl. oz (25-50ml) freshly-pressed raw carrot juice or other vegetable juice, or tomato juice.
   Large mixed raw salad. A few raisins or pieces of orange or apple can be added if liked, and a piece of an avocado pear, or sprouted grains, with a little grated or cottage cheese and a dressing of lemon juice and vegetable oil or herbs or home-made salad dressing.
   100 per cent wholewheat bread and butter.
   Follow, if liked, with a ripe banana and a few dates, or oatcakes and butter and honey, or a slice of homemade fruit cake or treacle biscuits.
   Milk to drink at the end if desired.
   (After this meal it is a good idea to have a short lying down rest if at all tired.)

Mid-afternoon:

Any of the drinks already suggested, or *weak* tea preferably without sugar.

Preferably nothing to eat unless the evening meal is some hours away and the mother feels hungry, when fruit or a salad sandwich may be taken.

Evening meal:

Grapefruit or vegetable soup or a small salad *hors d'oeuvres*.

Protein dish (cheese, nuts, lentils, soya, eggs, beans or peas, meat or fish if not a vegetarian).

Two or more lightly cooked vegetables, and possibly, if no indigestion, a potato baked in its skin, followed by fruit in some form or fruit salad with a little junket or yogurt or cream or baked egg custard.

Bedtime drink:

Any of the drinks previously suggested. May well be taken in bed.

Coffee:

Coffee contains caffeine which is not good for a growing embryo, so in place of ordinary coffee it is better to have a de-caffeinated coffee, or a coffee substitute such as *Pioneer*.

General Suggestions

1. If tired or not hungry, it may be wisest to miss a meal and just have one of the drinks suggested and then a good rest on the bed.
2. All food should be eaten slowly, and very well chewed.
3. Meals should not be rushed, but eaten with enjoyment.
4. Meals are generally best eaten dry, with drinks between times. Milk is really a food, and can be sipped as part of a meal.
5. Highly spiced foods, fried foods and twice-cooked foods and fancy cakes and pastries are best avoided, nor should foods be over-salted.

Natural Food Supplements

The diet suggested here provides the mother with an excellent range of essential nutrients, but it may sometimes be a good plan for her to include in her meals some of the natural food supplements that are extra rich in some valuable nutrients. One or more of the following supplements may be helpful, especially if a mother is particularly tired.

1. *Fresh, untreated wheatgerm:* 1-2 dessertspoonsful daily. Provides B and E vitamins, protein and mineral salts.
2. *Unprocessed bran:* Provides valuable fibre and is the best treatment for any tendency to constipation.
3. *Molasses or black treacle:* may be taken on bread and butter or as a drink in hot water. Provides potassium, calcium, magnesium, iron and phosphorus.
4. *Kelp:* seaweed. Contains mineral salts, especially iodine and potassium. One or more tablets daily, or use as a sprinkling on food.
5. *Bonemeal:* source of mineral salts. One tablet a day is advocated by Dr Aslander for laying the foundations for good teeth.

Smoking and Alcohol

Nicotine from smoking is damaging for the developing embryo and can lead to babies being born underweight and so at risk. It is not filtered out by the placenta as are many undesirable substances, so expectant mothers should not smoke during pregnancy.

Alcohol is not filtered out either, and it can also sometimes damage the embryo, so it is wisest generally to avoid alcohol.

As both smoking and alcohol are nowadays part of our social customs, cutting them out may entail a bit of effort, but most mothers will be glad to make the effort needed to do without them for her baby's sake. If an expectant mother has been a smoker, it can be a great help to her in giving it up if her husband also gives up smoking.

Summary of Dietary Principles

1. Choose wholefoods as far as possible (e.g. wholewheat bread).
2. Have a great deal of ripe raw fruit.
3. Have lots of fresh vegetables, and some raw salad each day.
4. Make good use of dairy produce.

5. Have adequate, good protein but not necessarily meat.
6. Choose organically grown foods if available.

As far as possible they should try to avoid eating:

1. Devitalized carbohydrate foods – particularly white bread and white sugar – and all the many biscuits, cakes, soft drinks and sweets made with them.
2. Over-processed foods, foods containing non-nutritious chemical additives as artificial colours and artificial flavours etc.

White bread and white sugar are the two major deficiency foods of modern civilization, and should be avoided by expectant mothers.
However, small amounts may sometimes have to be included for social reasons.

Dental Decay
Dental decay is one of the major ills of modern civilization, but the right foods during pregnancy and breast-feeding can do a great deal to reduce it. The Ministry of Health in their 'Dental Health' leaflet (H.M.S.O. 8/62, 20/62) says, 'Proper nutrition during pregnancy, infancy and childhood is important in building sound teeth. From the time weaning commences, the young child should be trained to eat savoury foods and wholegrain cereals.' Clearly mothers have a great opportunity here. The dentist can fill the holes in a child's teeth after they have come, but mothers can do a great deal to prevent many of the holes from ever appearing.

Making the Changes
Making the changes suggested here should not be too difficult for most mothers, especially if the father is actively helpful. It is never too late to begin to follow these suggestions, but it is best if they can be begun early, or even before conception actually takes place.

Water
Pure, fresh water is an excellent drink for expectant mothers, and sometimes it may be worthwhile buying bottled mountain water and drinking a glassful each day.

Raspberry Leaf Tea

An infusion made from raspberry leaves is a traditional drink for expectant mothers, especially during the last three months, and can be taken as a drink either morning or afternoon.

Sunshine

We accept sunshine and air so casually that sometimes we forget that it is essential for all life.

Sunshine is particularly important for expectant mothers. One of the advantages of raw food is that the mother takes into her system the stored sunshine in the plant that she eats, and she also will benefit from the direct effect of sunshine on her own body. Part of the sun's value can be stored for some months by the human body through the action of the sun's rays on the skin. This is most valuable, so expectant mothers should form the habit of having frequent short sun baths when the weather is favourable. The skin should be protected from over-exposure. Sunny air is also very beneficial and on very hot days it may be best to 'sunbathe in the shade'.

Fresh Air

The whole body needs a constant and ample supply of fresh air through the lungs and also on the skin. Deep breathing and air baths for the whole body should be an essential part of an expectant mother's regular daily routine, whether a sun bath is possible or not. It is also desirable to sleep with the windows open, so that the mother gets fresh air during the night; though if foggy, it would probably be better to leave them closed. Unfortunately our air may be polluted by lead from car exhausts, and lead is bad for babies and children, so here is a strong case for drastically reducing, or entirely disallowing, the addition of lead to petrol.

3.

Elimination

Good elimination of the body's waste products is the essential complement to good diet, and the human body is well supplied with the means for doing this.

There are four regular channels for eliminating body wastes:

1. Bowels
2. Kidneys
3. Lungs
4. Skin

These each have their own specific job, but they interact with each other too.

Bowels

If the wastes are not regularly removed, then the person suffers from constipation, and constipation leads to an impure blood stream, and may lead to a poor complexion, tiredness, headaches and so on. The taking of laxative drugs does secure an evacuation but is not as effective as a good diet in keeping the blood clean and healthy.

An expectant mother should make a habit of having a good free evacuation at least once a day.

Kidneys

The kidneys filter out the water and wastes collected by the blood as it circulates the body. Normally they can do this easily.

An expectant mother should have her urine examined at regular intervals to make sure that the kidneys are functioning normally and not being overloaded.

Lungs

The blood carries oxygen from the lungs to all the different cells and collects carbon dioxide from each of them, which it exchanges in the lungs for the oxygen, and the unwanted carbon dioxide leaves the body as the air is breathed out.

Expectant mothers, particularly, need lots of oxygen, and so each day they should do some deep breathing by a wide open window morning and evening and also acquire the habit of breathing deeply at other times too to expand their lung capacity.

The Skin

The skin is often forgotten as an organ of elimination, but it is actually an important one, being covered all over with tiny pores, or sweat glands, which are continually collecting and excreting water in which waste materials are dissolved. The minute traces of waste materials it carries may remain deposited on the skin, so you should have a quick wash or shower in warm water each day, followed perhaps by a cold shower if well tolerated.

Expectant mothers should keep their skin active and in good condition by daily contact with fresh air, and sun baths when possible, and by a daily morning friction rub, with a dry (or wet) loofa, or a rough towel.

While these four channels of elimination are important for everyone, they are particularly important for expectant mothers, who, though they do not need to 'eat for two', do need to eliminate for two, if they are to be in the best of health for the confinement, and give their baby the best start in life.

Clothing

An expectant mother's clothing is important too, and is associated with the work of the skin. It should fulfil the following functions:

1. Let the skin remain well aired.
2. Keep her warm and comfortable.
3. Avoid any pressure or constriction.
4. Look nice.

It is a good idea to wear a cellular cotton garment next to the skin, such as aertex or sea island cotton rather than nylon.

All constricting bands are undesirable, and skirts or jeans can be suspended from the shoulders, either on a bodice or with straps, and a loose tunic worn over them, so that the mother has no constriction round her waist. The 'Mothercare' catalogue can help with maternity wear. (See *Useful Addresses*.)

Shoes

Shoes should be wide enough to be comfortable, and should have low heels. Such shoes are best for walking, and a daily walk is an excellent plan during pregnancy.

Maternity Corsets

A girl's own abdominal muscles are the best possible support for the developing pregnancy, but if these muscles have been allowed to grow weak and flabby by lack of adequate exercise, they may not be able to do this job properly during pregnancy. If, in the latter months, there seems to be a need for some extra support, then properly designed maternity corsets may be worn if advised by the doctor.

4.

Morning Sickness

Morning sickness, or nausea, is not inevitable in pregnancy, and it seems to be considerably less common than it used to be, though it may still be a distressing accompaniment of some pregnancies. It is worst in the first three months, after which most expectant mothers will be free of it, but in some cases it may last for longer. On the other hand, some mothers have no nausea at all, or have it so slightly that it passes off as soon as they have had their breakfast. Modifications of the diet, extra rest and a happy cheerful outlook can do much to overcome the nausea, but drugs should *not* be taken for it. This is important, because nausea occurs mainly in the first three months of pregnancy, and it is in the first three months that the tiny embryo is most susceptible to damage from drugs taken by the mother, which may cross the placenta and reach the embryo.

Some people have found that a drink of a herb tea, first thing, while still in bed, helps them, but this does not go to the root of the trouble, which includes what the mother ate the day, or days before. The tendency still seems to be to regard nausea as an unavoidable accompaniment of pregnancy, but there is no justification for this fatalistic attitude, and it is often possible to alleviate it or even overcome it, especially by modifying her diet.

Pregnancy initiates a new set of processes, and there may be some hypersensitiveness in the digestive system, so that nausea may sometimes be the mother's system protesting against the meals that she has been having. This could mean that the mother needs to lighten the stresses on her digestion by having simpler meals. Potatoes baked in their skins have been found to be very good friends to mothers suffering from nausea, eaten by themselves, or with some steamed or conservatively cooked carrots or sprouts.

According to Dr Howard Hay, starches and sugars should not be eaten at the same meal as protein, and acid fruits should not be eaten with starch foods. Lightly cooked vegetables and raw vegetable salads can, he says, be eaten with any other foods, and so generally can milk. His principles can be very helpful in some cases of morning sickness. Any mother with morning sickness also needs to have less of the solid acid-producing foods such as meat, bread, cakes or sweets, and more of the vitalizing, alkaline foods such as fruits and vegetables. Her stomach might be able to deal quite well with a simple meal of carrots, brussels sprouts and grated cheese, followed by a ripe eating apple or pear, when a more orthodox meal of meat and two vegetables followed by apple pie and custard would prove to be too much for it, bringing on nausea next day.

Fasting

If the sickness is severe, then it can be helpful to try having one or two days of complete abstinence from all food, and just live on water and diluted fruit or vegetable juices and clear vegetable broth, having as many drinks as wanted, possibly a glassful of one or other of the drinks every hour. While doing this it will probably be necessary to take a good aperient drink first thing and/or some bran tablets.

In addition the mother can take a tea-cupful of gentian root tea* two or three times a day. This can be very effective in cutting the nausea, and can be taken regularly even if not fasting.

Precautions to Minimize Morning Sickness

1. Constipation

Any tendency to constipation should be overcome, as it can easily be a factor in morning sickness as well as other disabilities. The best way to avoid it is to have plenty of roughage from fruits and vegetables and also from 100 per cent wholewheat bread. One may also add two or more teaspoonsful of unprocessed bran to breakfast, or as much as

* Consult your doctor before taking this herb.

is needed to secure a daily soft and regular motion. Processed breakfast bran cereals do not seem to be as effective as the unprocessed bran.

2. Tiredness

Sometimes nausea is simply due to doing too much and to lack of adequate rest, so extra rest and complete relaxation should be included in treating morning sickness. A midday rest is often very helpful, and early to bed should be the rule.

3. Deep Breathing

This is important as it secures plenty of oxygen in the blood to keep it healthy.

4. Atmosphere

Stuffy atmospheres should be avoided as they can produce nausea.

5. Smoking

Being in a smoke laden room may induce nausea and, if so, it should be avoided. It can be bad for the embryo.

6. Cooking Smells

Sometimes, the smell of cooking will induce nausea but, if it is unavoidable, it may be a case of 'grin and bear it'.

7. Incompatible Mixtures

Avoiding these may seem a bit of a nuisance but it helps some people.

8. Fats and Fatty Foods

Such foods should be kept to a minimum and fried foods omitted.

9. Occupation

It helps the mother to be occupied and, if she already has a toddler, looking after him can help by taking her mind off her own sensations.

5.

Second Fundamental: Athletic Training

In no field of athletics is a great event undertaken without proper training, and a woman embarking on the genuinely athletic event of giving birth to a baby should have appropriate training for the job too. The aim of training for a birth is particularly to help the mother co-operate actively in the second stage of expelling the baby, partly by controlled breathing and also to learn how to relax, when appropriate, to let the muscles get on with their job unrestricted.

The aim of the athletic training is to increase the flexibility and elasticity of the muscles concerned rather than to give them very great strength. Some of the muscles used at the birth are used for this particular function only, and others are only slightly used in other activities, so that it is important to tone them all up by suitable exercises in advance. If the muscles are weak and flabby difficulties in the birth are only to be expected.

As the abdomen increases in size, the skin and underlying tissues become stretched and, to help them to keep their elasticity and regain their normal appearances after the birth, the whole abdomen should be massaged with a vegetable oil each day from about the third month. This will help to protect the mother from unsightly stretch scars sometimes left after a birth.

Training for a birth should include practice in deep breathing and in complete relaxation, and in trained breathing for labour.

The ability to relax when necessary is important, for some of the pains of childbirth have been attributed, notably by Dr Dick Read, to tension and fear (see p.68). It is not necessary to do a long period of exercises each day, but just a few minutes done regularly. Some useful exercises are given here, but it is really best, if possible, to join some ante-natal classes, either as suggested by one's doctor, or classes organized by the National Childbirth Trust. One should begin gradually, and never tire oneself or try to do too many at a time.

Ante-natal Exercises

These exercises should be done without any strain, in an easy rhythmical way, but not on the first three days when a period would have been due, without the experts approval. Breathing and relaxation can however, be practised on these days. Always stop if beginning to feel tired. It is a good plan just to confirm the exercises with your doctor or clinic.

1. *Lie Flat on the Back on the Floor*
   (a) Slowly bend the right knee up towards the abdomen, then stretch out the leg and lower to the floor. Repeat three or four times.
   (b) Same exercise with the left leg.
   (c) Same exercise with both legs moving alternatively in a smooth slow motion (like cycling). Rest, letting the whole body go limp, then do three deep breaths. Relax completely.

2. *Stand Erect*
   (a) Feet together, rise on toes breathing in.
   (b) Bend the knees and go down to a squatting position, breathing out and supporting the position with both hands on some firm object.
   (c) Open the knees as wide as possible, breathing in.
   (d) Close the knees breathing out.
   (e) Repeat.
   (f) Raise the body.
   (g) Lower the heels and relax. This exercise may be repeated with the heels apart. Relax and breathe deeply.

3. *Kneel on Floor on Hands and Knees, Knees and Hands Apart*
  - (a) Drop head and lift up the back, raising all the internal organs as much as possible, breathing in.
  - (b) Raise the hand, and hollow the back by raising the buttocks, breathing out. Repeat, sit on the floor and relax.

4. *Standing, Lying Down or Sitting*
  - (a) Press the buttocks hard together.
  - (b) Press the thighs together.
  - (c) Pull up vagina and bladder as though trying not to pass water. Hold and relax. Repeat.

5. *Tip Toe Walking*
  - (a) Rise on the toes.
  - (b) Taking little steps, walk round the room, rest, and repeat.

6. *Exercises for the Neck*
  - (a) Drop the head forward as far as possible on to the chest.
  - (b) Rotate the head slowly over the right shoulder.
  - (c) Continue rotating backwards dropping the head as far back as possible.
  - (d) Continue rotating round to left and forward again onto the chest.
  - (e) Raise the head to normal position and rest. Repeat, turning first to the left and repeat both ways.

Deep Breathing and the Diaphragm

Between the thorax and the abdomen there is a muscular structure that divides the body into two parts. It is a very important muscle, and should be used in deep breathing. Systems of physical training have been based on the diaphragm, and its proper functioning was one of the secrets of the Greeks' poise and physical perfection.

1. *Controlled Deep Breathing*
  - (a) Lie flat on the back.
  - (b) Breathe in, filling the abdomen.
  - (c) Continue breathing in, expanding the chest, and the ribs sideways.

(d) Breathe out slowly, contracting the abdomen walls and drawing the diaphragm in and upwards.

(e) Rest without breathing in again for a few seconds. Repeat these deep breaths five times.

2. *Deep Breathing at Odd Moments*
Take ten short breaths in, without breathing out, and then one long breath out, breathing both in and out through the nose. This may be done when walking out of doors, or during housework.

Sleep

Sleep is the period when the body relaxes and can become refreshed and repaired, and it is especially desirable for an expectant mother to have plenty of good sleep because of the double function that her body is carrying out. The type of diet, coupled with exercise and fresh air as here suggested, will help to promote deep and refreshing sleep. Most mothers will benefit from going to bed in good time, and having a long night's sleep. Lack of sleep and late nights may result in morning sickness, tiredness or irritability, so a normal routine of going to bed at about 10 p.m. will benefit most mothers. With adequate sleep, it is amazing how energetic and full of vitality a woman can feel throughout her pregnancy.

Sometimes, in the later months, a mother may find her sleep is interfered with because the baby inside her is restless, but it is often possible to effect some control over this restlessness by placing a hand gently over the baby and 'willing' him to lie still. She may also have to get up in the night to pass water, but should try to train herself to go straight off to sleep again by adopting a peaceful and relaxed frame of mind.

Rest

Adequate rest is an essential part of a mother's training, so she should make herself get enough, even if she feels she has too much to do to take a rest. Many mothers may benefit from having a daily lying down rest after their midday meal. Some mothers need this more than others do, but for most mothers it is a good plan to lie down and put the feet up even if only for half an hour. This is particularly beneficial if there is nausea, and such a rest can make a great difference to enjoyment of the second half of the day.

A High Stool

It is a good plan for expectant and nursing mothers to keep a high stool, possibly with a foot rest, in the kitchen, and to train themselves to sit on it for jobs such as washing up, preparing vegetables, ironing etc. At first this may seem to be more trouble than it is worth, but it is a habit well worth acquiring, and soon it becomes easy and natural to use it. Such a stool is particularly helpful in cases of varicose veins or a dropped uterus, if either of these should occur at any time, not only during pregnancy.

Relaxation

As a definite part of her training programme, and as a supplement to ordinary rest, the mother should acquire the habit of complete relaxation. To be able to relax at will is invaluable both when tired or unable to get to sleep, but especially at the time of the birth itself. One way of learning to relax is to lie on one's bed and take a deep breath clenching the fists and tensing all one's muscles, hold this for a few moments and let all the breath go fairly quickly, letting every muscle in the body lose its tension; so relaxed, in fact, that if an arm or leg is raised by a friend and then let go, it just flops back to the bed like a lifeless rag doll.

As an alternative, to start with one may consciously go over each part of the body, telling each one in one's mind that they are relaxed and 'floppy', beginning with the eyes, mouth, neck, right hand, lower arm, upper arm, shoulders, left hand and arm, chest, back, abdomen and the parts of each leg in turn, so that the whole body feels as if it were falling down into the bed. During the birth there should be a rhythm of muscular activity followed by a period of complete relaxation, as this facilitates an easy birth.

Posture

Correct posture is a way of continuing to exercise throughout the day. When standing, ideally the abdominal muscles should be holding the internal organs back and slightly up into the proper places and the buttocks should be 'tucked in', so as to reduce the amount of curve in the back. If the small of the back is hollowed and the buttocks stick out behind, an ugly posture results, often with the shoulders slumped forward as well. Instead, the head and shoulders should be held up in a good position, and this, in itself, tends to induce a feeling of well being.

Walking and Gardening

In addition to the regular exercises, a brisk daily walk of, if possible about half an hour, is very beneficial, as it stirs up the whole system and brings fresh air into the lungs and blood stream. Gardening is also generally a good occupation for expectant mothers for it exercises various muscles, and keeps her in the fresh air. If she can grow some of her own vegetables organically, this is an added advantage.

Position for Evacuation of the Bowels

There is one excellent piece of daily training that every expectant mother can consider doing. This is to give up using the ordinary lavatory seat and use a chamber pot instead, the pot being kept in the lavatory. The mother then, several times a day, will be automatically exercising just those muscles which are concerned with the birth itself, muscles which normally get little use. She need not actually sit on the chamber, but can just squat over it with hands on chair for support if wanted. One of the reasons for the easy births of women who live in more primitive conditions is said to be the fact that they do not use lavatory seats, but just squat to pass faeces and urine.

Ten Commandments for Mothers-to-be

1. Choose the right kinds of high quality natural foods.
2. Avoid eating over-processed and over-sophisticated poor quality foods.
3. See that waste materials are regularly and efficiently eliminated.
4. Have lots of sunshine and fresh air.

5. Give up smoking and alcohol.
6. Take adequate daily exercise.
7. Learn to relax and have plenty of good sleep.
8. Wear loose clothes and low-heeled shoes.
9. Cultivate a joyous outlook free from fears or worries.
10. Remember that giving birth is an absolutely normal function, for which a woman's body is beautifully and marvellously designed.

6.

Third Fundamental: Spiritual Outlook

We know that the influence of the mind over the body is considerable, and during pregnancy, when all the mother's functions and emotions are highly sensitized, this influence may be enhanced. This means that the mother's spiritual outlook and her mental and emotional attitude are important in maintaining her health and happiness while she is carrying her baby and during the birth itself. Too little attention may have been given to this side of pregnancy, but it does merit being called the Third Fundamental for producing a perfect and healthy baby in a simple and natural way.

Babies have certain rights, and a baby's first essential right is the right to be *wanted*. It makes a difference to the baby as well as to the mother if the baby is wanted, and the luckiest babies are those who are actively wanted by both parents before conception even takes place. Generally, however, even if the baby may not have been actively desired in the first place, when the mother finds that she is pregnant she usually cheerfully adapts herself mentally and accepts the facts as they are, and decides to do everything that she can for her growing baby.

Not all mothers feel a rush of love the moment that their baby is born. They should not worry, but should wait and let their love grow naturally as they care for their baby and get to know him.

Spiritual Forces
When carrying her unborn baby a woman may feel herself to

be a part of the great creative and spiritual forces of the world, at times on a plane somewhat apart from the rest of humanity. It is a time when one may feel capable of 'tuning in to the infinite'. To have a baby is a deeply rooted desire among women, and in spite of all the other attractions and opportunities life now offers to women, there is still this heartfelt urge to have babies.

When her baby comes first in her mind and heart, it makes it easier for an expectant mother to follow the beneficial regime of right diet, rest, fresh air and exercise previously outlined. Any smoking, late nights, drinks parties etc. which previously contributed to her recreations lose their charm if they would be detrimental to her baby whose welfare has become a first priority. If a mother does not accept the facts of her pregnancy, and adapt her life accordingly, but tries to go on as she did before, then conflict may arise, with the possibility of aggravating sickness, tiredness, irritability and emotional disturbances. Conflict, especially a repressed conflict, is undesirable during pregnancy.

If a mother's heart is full of confidence because she knows that she is doing the things that will make her baby healthy and the birth natural, and for which her body is so marvellously designed, and if her heart is also full of love and joy at the thought of her coming motherhood, then there will be little if any room for worry or anxiety but only for joy and contentment. If emotional difficulties do sometimes occur, this is usually only when the mother has become over-tired or has failed to adapt herself fully to the idea of having a baby. A little more rest, a little more sunshine and fresh air, and a little extra love from her husband will usually overcome any emotional upset or depression.

Anxiety and Fear

In the past, some expectant mothers suffered from fears or anxieties about pain and difficulties of birth, but knowledge of the facts, and confidence in what she is doing to promote a natural birth and a perfect baby are the best ways to avoid or banish such feelings. If fears should persist, then talking about them to a sympathetic but sensible friend, (or perhaps, a

National Childbirth Counsellor), and concentrating on the thought that birth is not designed to be painful, will generally help a great deal.

Besides upsetting the happiness of the waiting period, fear has a bad effect on the birth itself. Dr Dick Read found that when a mother is suffering from fear during the birth of her baby, while one set of the muscles of the uterus is working to push the baby out, another set, which should be relaxed, is tense and contracting, and will be working against the first set. According to him it is this working of the muscles against each other which can be the cause of excessive pain, and is not anything inherent in birth itself.

Dr Read quotes a case of his where he watched a native girl have a simple natural birth without fear, and apparently without pain. Of the girl, who conducted the birth by herself, he says, 'Elation, wonder, tenderness and the pride of creation appeared to combine in a great storm of pleasing emotions, and with their influence the birth of a child had been completed.' This is what birth should be like, and it is tragic that our civilization has deprived so many women of what could and should be happy and joyful birth experiences.

This kind of natural, easy birth is what we want to aim at, and we should be able to get back to it if we make proper ante-natal preparations and replace fears with confidence and joy. If a woman does not quite reach this stage, she should be helped by the knowledge that the doctor can, should she desire it, give her a whiff or two of gas to take the edge off any pain if it seems to be getting too severe.

Pre-selection of Sex

Sometimes a mother will set her heart on having either a boy or a girl, so it is as well to know that the sex of the baby is determined at the moment of conception, and is, at present, still a matter of chance, depending on whether the one sperm out of the thousands present at the time of conception is one carrying male or female characteristics.

Young mothers are wisest to concentrate on producing a healthy and happy baby, and not to worry about the sex, as it is hard on the baby if the mother sets her heart on having a girl, and a boy arrives or vice-versa.

A New Profession to be Learnt

During the months of her first pregnancy there are lots of things for the new mother to learn about babies and children, as regards their physical, emotional and psychological development and their training, and about the profession of Motherhood. Motherhood is a grand profession, and should be treated as such by the community. Girls who give up a well-paid job and choose to make Motherhood and caring for their home their full-time professional career and their top priority, should receive the respect and admiration of other women. There can hardly be a better or more worthwhile job than working for the health and happiness of the next generation.

Mothers should never be regarded as, in some way, second class citizens, which sometimes seems to be the attitude of the more extreme advocates of women's rights. Nor can Motherhood be relegated to the status of being a sort of hobby or a side line, if its full joys are to be experienced by the parents, and if the baby is to have the best possible start in life, based on his parents love and care.

Much has been done to give women a fairer deal in the world today, and many women now do marvellous jobs of which they can feel justly proud; but this fairer deal should also include upgrading *womanhood*, and the unique function of Motherhood, so that women can also feel justly proud of being good mothers.

Mothers Who Work Outside their Homes

Before the Baby is Born

If an expectant mother has a job which she likes, and is feeling fit, there is no need to feel that she should give it up immediately. Each individual will vary, so there can be no actual rules. As guidelines, however, a mother should not carry on with a job if it makes her feel over-tired, or feel that she is too weary to bother to make the right foods for herself, or that she does not have the time to do her ante-natal exercises, breathing practice, and relaxation, or to attend her ante-natal classes. Nor should financial considerations induce her to continue with a job if it is over-tiring her. Part-time work, if available, can sometimes be a good idea.

During the last four to six weeks it is usually considered wisest to give up any outside jobs, and to concentrate more on preparing for the coming baby.

Since most girls have a paid job before they are married – sometimes a highly-paid professional job – it is only natural for them to want to continue with such work after they are married for mental satisfaction as well as for financial reasons.

As a matter of common sense and good management, it would generally seem wisest for a good part of the wife's earnings to be spent on capital goods for the home, or to be saved up for a potential family, while the regular expenses of running the home are financed out of the husband's earnings. In this way, the cessation of the wife's income with the advent of a baby will be unlikely to entail too great an alteration in the family's standard of living.

After the Baby is Born

When there is a baby, the work situation is different and for the baby's early years there is a strong case for mothers to give up any outside job, and to regard their baby and home as their career. The profession of Motherhood is one of the most important jobs that women can undertake and can be a most satisfying and rewarding one, in spite of its various restrictions when the babies are small. It can be an interesting and rewarding job throughout childhood, employing a wide range of talents with many interests. As their children get older, some mothers may well want to go back to some work outside their home, for the satisfaction of their job and for the fun and companionship of working at some job in a community of other workers, as well as for the extra money for their family.

If this results in 'latch key' children, however, it may not be worth it. Only if a mother can get reliable, full-time help will it be reasonable for her to take a full-time job while her baby is small, but there is inevitably still some price to be paid for this, as babies do need their own mothers.

Mothers at Home

Children do so much need to have their mother around when she is wanted:

– to be shown the first spring flower

– to help to bury the little dead sparrow
– to wash the cut knee
– to make the refractory toy work
– to answer the endless questions
– to mend the broken doll
– to make the birthday cake and tie the party bow
– to provide the feeling of security that the knowledge of her *availability* gives them.

In brief, she needs to be there to express her love and interest for her children in all the little practical ways which may seem so trivial but which, in the aggregate, mean so much, and which help to build up a worthwhile relationship between them.

To have no domestic help, and to be tied to the house and children for years can bring about a sense of loneliness and frustration which are extremely bad for anyone to have to endure, but many young mothers unite to form playgroups or toddlers clubs which do a great deal for the babies and toddlers and help to reduce the loneliness of the mothers who can make new friends.

7.

The Father

Few things have changed more radically in recent years than has the function of the father during his wife's pregnancy and the birth of his baby. In the past, many fathers must have felt a bit superfluous at the birth and spent too much time being worried and anxious, but nowadays, instead of being something of an outsider, father can not only participate in the expectant mother's ante-natal preparations but also be present at the birth itself.

There are ante-natal meetings for fathers, where they can learn much about pregnancy and birth and these are very well patronized by expectant fathers. If husband and wife both desire it, the father can be with his wife throughout labour and can see his baby actually being born. This is a marvellous experience, and can be of inestimable benefit to both parents, and for the baby and for the creation of a new family unit, with husband and wife being partners from the very beginning in the new venture of parenthood. The fact that her husband will be with her during the birth is an added incentive to the mother to do everything she can in advance to ensure that the birth of their baby will be a simple and natural one in which she herself is consciously participating.

The father's knowledge of what is going on, and his interest, sympathy and help to his wife over her routine, diet and exercises can be invaluable. If she is sometimes a bit over-tired or depressed, he can be a tower of strength and comfort, since his knowledge gives him understanding of what she is experiencing.

There are, of course, many practical and helpful jobs that the father can take on in their new joint responsibilities, not only just helping with the normal household chores, but, if he is a handyman, there will be various jobs that he can do in preparing the baby's room, or corner, in the way of putting up shelves or a drying rack or making a screen to go round the baby's cot. If he has an interest in gardening, then he could make compost and grow vegetables organically for his wife. Brussels sprouts can be especially valuable, as they can be chopped up and used raw in winter salads as fresh green food.

Also, he can help his wife by giving up smoking if he normally smokes.

Food and Regime

It is a great asset if the husband helps his wife to follow a good regime and have a wise diet of high quality natural foods by having the same kind of foods himself, as far as is reasonable. If she is being a vegetarian, he can still have meat if he wants to, but can join her in not having fancy sugary foods. He can help by being ready to eat the salads and vegetables and fruits and wholegrain bread that should form a major part of her meals. He can encourage her to do her exercises, and to practice the N.C.T. special breathing exercises for labour.

He can also help her to avoid stuffy places of entertainment, late nights or a too exciting social life, being prepared to leave a party early, to take his wife home – although, of course, some form of social activity is an advantage. He may be able to arrange to have special leave, or to take some of his annual holiday when his wife first comes out of hospital, so that he can look after her and the baby and also the toddler, if there is one.

Intercourse

Intercourse during pregnancy is something that each individual couple can best decide for themselves, with the advice of their doctor and guided by mutual love and sympathy, and especially by what the wife feels about it. If there is a history of miscarriage it may well be wisest to refrain from intercourse during the first three months of pregnancy, particularly on the first two or three days when a period would have been due. Again, in the last month the couple may decide to omit it.

After the birth, feelings about intercourse vary, and though some mothers may feel ready for it quite soon, others may not, perhaps not for some weeks. If the mother is still tired, or sore after stitches, then making love with just gentle caressing but without actual intercourse may be the answer.

The mother's feelings about it will be the best guide as to the frequency of intercourse during breast-feeding.

Finance

The financial side of having a baby is very much the father's concern and, if money is short, it may be a good plan to have a special savings scheme whereby so much is set aside each week for the baby's account, the amount depending on his and his wife's income.

The father may also like to consider taking out some extra insurance, such as an Educational Policy or 'cover' policy. With, say, a twenty-year cover policy, a man can pay a small additional premium on top of his normal life insurance policy, and by this, he ensures to his wife, should he die, an annual income for any part of the twenty years left after his death. This means that, should he die while his children are small, his wife will have an annual income considerably greater than he could afford under normal insurance schemes, but, if he does not die within the twenty years, she gets a lump sum, but no annual income. This can be a very valuable type of insurance for the young man with a relatively small income.

After the Baby is Born

Once the baby is born there is great happiness, and it is one of the father's jobs to notify friends and relatives and to put the birth in the paper and to register the birth. The father should know that the establishment of breast-feeding is a first priority, over which his support can be most helpful. While the mother is not an invalid, she should not try to do too much too quickly. Having a baby should not impair a woman's health or figure, but she may need a little extra rest at first to facilitate successful breast-feeding. It will also be useful because of the extra work the general care of her baby will automatically bring. The new father can take some of the work of the home off his wife's shoulders, but on the other hand a young mother has to remember that her husband may have a heavy job, and she should not presume on his willingness to help.

Modern young fathers are often very expert in handling their new baby even when he is very tiny, and in this way the baby endears himself to his father. Changing nappies and bathing the baby need not be a job for mothers only, if the father is willing to participate in this part of babycare, and parenthood.

The Toddler

There is one job which is particularly the father's responsibility, if it is not the first child, which is to give love and reassurance to the toddler, as the arrival of a new baby will inevitably mean some alterations in the previous order and security of his life. His father can see that order and security are still there and can also ensure that the toddler shall feel part of the extended family, and that the new baby is also 'his', and is someone whom he wants to welcome and give a lot of love to.

8.

General Preparations for Mother and Baby

If expecting a guest, one prepares the guest room with clean sheets and so on. In the same way a young wife intending to have a baby should try to ensure that she is in really good health herself before starting this important job. If she suffers from constipation, colds or catarrh, then a few days of eating only fresh fruit with bran to make sure that she has no constipation, and diluted fruit juices to drink, can be a very good plan.

Teeth and Hair
Decayed teeth can be a source of discomfort as well as being a potential danger to expectant mothers, so a visit to the dentist should form part of the mother's ante-natal preparations, so that any decayed teeth can be treated, and any necessary fillings completed. Dental treatment is free for expectant mothers and for a year after the birth. If an extraction should be found to be desirable after conception has taken place, the doctor's advice should be sought, as a general anaesthetic in the early months of pregnancy may not be desirable.

She should also take good care of her hair, washing and brushing it regularly and, if it is permed, she may like to consider having a fresh perm before the expected birth, as there will be little time for it after and she will want to look nice when having her baby.

Inverted Nipples
Normally, the breasts develop as pregnancy advances, so that after the baby is born the breasts are ready to secrete milk.

Just occasionally the nipples may be depressed or inverted and, if this is the case, then the doctor may agree that the nipples should be very gently drawn out each day, possibly with a breast pump, and very gently rolled between the finger and thumb, with a little olive oil or lanolin on the fingers. The nipple will then eventually remain out, and the baby will do the rest.

Signs of Pregnancy

The first sign that pregnancy has started is usually the cessation of the monthly periods, and then the breasts may begin to enlarge, and there may be a bit of morning sickness. If not already having a good diet of whole fresh foods, the mother should start immediately to have the kind of meals outlined in Chapter 2, and she should also do daily exercises, special breathing exercises and practice relaxation. If she has not already got a doctor, she should set about choosing one, making enquiries among her friends to find a suitable doctor – one who is interested in, and sympathetic towards, natural births and to mental and physical training for childbirth, and who has a reputation for being good with children. The easier and more friendly her relations with her doctor, the easier it will be for her to discuss things with him/her and also to discuss the conduct of the confinement.

Once her pregnancy has been confirmed, she will be expected to visit her doctor once a month, and probably to bring a urine specimen with her, to help her doctor check up that all is well. Regular attendance at a baby clinic or hospital for check ups and for exercise classes, or National Childbirth Trust classes, is most important throughout pregnancy for the health of both mother and baby right from the beginning.

After the third period has been missed, the doctor may give the mother an internal examination, which is quite simple, and is again a means by which her doctor will make sure that everything is normal. She will also receive a certificate from her doctor which she takes to her local Social Security office who will give her leaflet NI 17A which gives her particulars of maternity benefits.

Where to Have the Baby

Ideally, if mothers want it, it should be possible to have the baby at home, but this is not always easy, for though there are still many qualified midwives who could help to carry out home births with 'low risk' mothers, doctors, do not, as a rule favour home births, as they like to know that if by any chance there should be some difficulty over the birth all the best hospital facilities would be immediately available.

Anyone who very much desires to have a home birth should try to find a doctor who would agree to take her on, and she should also write to the National Childbirth Trust for any information that they may have on the subject, and for their leaflet Home Confinements, or to the Society to Support Home Confinement (see Useful Addresses). There might be a 'flying ambulance' on call for home births, should expert help be needed or if the mother needed to be transferred to a hospital, but this is by no means universally available.

Whether the baby is born at home or in hospital, some resident home help, or the father on paternity leave, if possible, is desirable for the first week or so after the mother goes home, as mothers are not kept for long in hospital these days – perhaps five or six days for a first baby, but as little as 48 hours for later babies, if the mother wants to go home, and satisfactory arrangements have been made.

The Hospital Stay

Mothers who have been having a natural type of diet, using wholewheat bread and whole, fresh foods generally, with a good proportion raw, may feel that hospital diet does not conform with what they have been having, but many hospitals do give the patients some helpful choices, and hospital diets are much better than they used to be. In any case, the mother should not worry, as worry will do her more harm than a more orthodox type of diet will for the short time that she will be in hospital. She can elect to be a vegetarian if she wants to and should ask for weak tea or coffee. She can take some useful supplements in with her, such as apples or other fruits, and a packet of wheatgerm (Bemax or Froment) and some unprocessed bran, so that she has no trouble with constipation. She could also take in a jar of honey, but she does not want to make a nuisance of herself.

The hospital will no doubt tell the mother what she needs to take in in the way of personal equipment for her stay in hospital, probably something in the order of two or three nightdresses suitable for breast-feeding, a nursing bra, dressing gown and slippers and a dressing jacket, washing and make-up equipment, etc.

Baby Equipment

Baby's Layette

The modern baby does not have long clothes, except perhaps wearing a long family robe for a christening.

'Mothercare' provides a wonderful selection of various clothes for babies and toddlers, and it is worthwhile ordering their catalogue, even if just for ideas (see *Useful Addresses*), and they have many shops around the country.

If making some of the clothes oneself, it is important to avoid tight bands and small armholes. An absorbent type of material is best next to the skin and some soft cotton material such as tropical aertex is ideal for little 'vests', which can be made on a magyar pattern with flat seams and bound edges.

One-piece knitted play suits are very useful and comfortable, but since modern designs and materials are so varied and enchanting each mother's selection will depend on individual choice and the finance available.

She will also need about twenty-four towel nappies. Most mothers now seem to use disposable nappy liners in place of muslin harrington nappies and, provided that these are changed frequently (after each feed), the current practice of using plastic over-pants does not seem to do any harm, and they are a boon for protecting the baby's clothes and bedding. A few soft harrington nappies are useful instead of a pillow and for 'mopping up'.

Cradle and Bedding

1. Cot or cradle on stand.
2. Possibly one enveloping blanket – about 6 ft by 4 ft placed under the mattress, and hanging over sides and the foot.
3. One mattress, usually covered with plastic material.
4. Two flannelette cot under-blankets.

5. One or two waterproof sheets.
6. Large Terry towel napkins or flannel sheets.
7. One or two soft fleecy nestling blankets – about 27 in by 36 in.
8. Coverlet of cellular material.

Pillows are not used and a soft harrington napkin can be folded for the baby's head to lie on.

The baby may be tucked up in a nestling blanket in the cot and then the sides of the enveloping blanket drawn over and the bottom lightly tucked in.

Screen

A screen (which can be made from a towel horse) is useful to put round the cot to keep draughts, (but not fresh air) away from the cradle or bath. The cradle should normally be near an open window.

Bathing Corner

It is nice to have a special bathing corner for the baby which could contain:

1. Low nursing chair without arms.
2. Gas or electric fire with fixed fireguard.
3. Bath on stand and jugs for water.
4. Baby soap and two flannels – one for face only.
5. Bottle of vegetable oil.
6. Two large soft towels.
7. Two soft muslin face towels.
8. Baby basket on stand or small table, with pockets round the sides, containing soft hair brush, rustless safety pins and pin cushion, screw-topped jar for cotton wool, receptacle for used cotton wool swabs, blunt-edged scissors, two small enamel basins and baby powder.
9. Two pails for used napkins (one for wet and one for soiled napkins).
10. All-purpose nursing apron for mother (see 'Mothercare').
11. Small clothes horse for airing clothes.
12. Small baby potty (optional).
13. Small chest for the baby's clothes and napkins.

All the baby's washing materials, towels, etc. must be kept for his exclusive use. After gently patting dry (*patting*, not rubbing) a little oil may be put in the creases, and on the buttocks and a little good baby powder can be used as desired.

The Pram
It is easiest for the mother to select the pram before the baby is born, even if it is not delivered until after the birth. Many types are available and the pram should have a brake and sun canopy. Some parents may choose a carry-cot on wheels for both day and night use, but in such cases it is essential for the bedding to be fully aired and changed as necessary morning and evening. Such cots may be too small for the baby at night after the first five months.

Play Pen
From the age of about four months the baby may use a play pen. If he gets used to this from an early age it is a great help to the busy mother, but he should not be left alone in it for too long or he may feel lonely and frustrated. After about twelve to fifteen months little use is usually made of it.

Carrying Sling
A special sling, for carrying the baby around and which leaves the mothers hands and arms free is a very useful piece of equipment and one which gives the baby pleasurable contact with his mother or father.

Baby's Rights

1. To be loved and wanted by both parents before and after birth.
2. To be wisely nurtured in the vital nine months before birth, with his mother providing food of the highest possible nutritional quality through her own food so as to ensure the right raw materials for a healthy mind and body, and for his mother also to have sunshine and fresh air.
3. To be born as easily and naturally as possible, preferably without the necessity of using instruments or drugs.

4. To be placed on his mother's bare abdomen immediately after birth to ensure the important 'maternal bonding'.
5. To be fed with his mother's milk, specially prepared for him, and *not to have anything else before this*.
6. To be accepted as a real personality always, from birth, and not first as a pet and later as a nuisance.
7. To be sympathetically helped to fit into the family life without being expected to reach too high a standard at too early an age.

9.

Before the Birth

If a mature egg-cell is present when intercourse takes place and sperms are deposited in the vagina, and make their way up into the uterus and tubes, one of the sperms may unite with the ovum and fertilize it. The sperms are microscopic, 1/300 inch in diameter, and can move about slowly. Thousands of them are present at each act of intercourse.

If a sperm does unite with the ovum, the fertilized ovum, smaller than a pin's head, may attach itself to the wall of the uterus and the new life starts to grow. The fertilized egg-cell is called the foetus. Its development is amazingly quick and elaborate, but, for the first few weeks, it remains absolutely tiny. The ovum, a single cell, first divides into two cells, which grow and divide again into four, eight, sixteen, thirty-two cells and so on.

Twins

Sometimes, when the fertilized ovum first divides into two cells, these separate instead of remaining together and both halves develop into babies, so that twins are formed ('identical' twins, always the same sex*). Twins may also develop if two ripe ova are present together and both become fertilized ('simultaneous twins', which may be of different sexes).

Details of Baby's Growth

At the End of Four Weeks
The foetus is about ½ in (1cm) long and weighs about 1/24 oz

---

*It is possible to insure against the extra expense of twins in the early months of pregnancy.

(1g). It is much curved, there are no limbs, and the head is larger than the body. No menstruation will have occurred.

At the End of Eight Weeks

The embryo is about 1 in (2.5cm) long and weighs 1/7 oz (4g). The head has a human shape, the eyes are prominent and nose and ears recognizable, but sex is not yet distinguishable. Arms and legs have begun to form. The embryo is floating in a bath of fluid which supports and protects it, in a bag inside the uterus. The fluid acts as a shock-absorber during pregnancy, and also helps to expand the mouth of the uterus at the birth.

The foetus is nourished through a cord, called the umbilical cord, which goes from its own navel to the wall of the uterus. There is no direct communication of blood from the mother's system. Her blood comes with food and oxygen to the uterus, and from the blood-vessels in its wall the food and oxygen are passed to the embryonic blood-stream. The exchange takes place in spongy tissue called the placenta, to which the umbilical cord is attached. In this way many poisonous substances which may be in the mother's blood, which are relatively harmless to her, but which would prove harmful to the developing embryo, are kept away from it.

Nicotine, and alcohol, however, both of which may be present in the mother's blood if she smokes, and takes alcoholic drinks, and both of which can damage the embryo, can pass with the food and oxygen from the tiny blood-vessels of the mother to the tiny blood-vessels of the embryo, as can also some drugs, e.g. thalidomide. Morning sickness may be present.

At the End of the Twelfth Week

The embryo is about 3¼ in (8cm) long and weighs just under 1 oz (25g). The eyelids are distinct, but short. The heart beats with force and miniature nails, fingers and toes are beginning to form. Sex organs can be distinguished. Morning sickness usually passes off.

At the End of the Sixteenth Week

The foetus is 5-6 in (13-15cm) long and weighs 4-6 oz (100-175g). The skin is covered with fine hair.

At the End of the Twentieth Week

The foetus is about 7-8 in (18-20cm) long and weighs about 8½ oz (240g). The head is very large in proportion to the body and the umbilical cord is about one foot (30cm) long. At about this stage the mother usually feels the baby's own movements in her womb. This is called the 'quickening' because in the olden days the baby was thought to start life at this stage.

At the End of the Twenty-fourth Week

The foetus is about 1 ft (30cm) long and weighs about 1½ lb (675g). It is very wrinkled, as there is as yet very little fat beneath the skin. It is possible to hear the heart beats very clearly with a stethoscope, and the doctor may give the stethoscope to the mother so that she can hear them herself. It is a thrilling sound.

At the End of the Twenty-eighth Week

The foetus is about 14½ in (37cm) long and weighs about 2½ lb (approx. 1 kg). The bony system is being completed. The eyes are open and eyelashes and eyebrows are beginning to form. If born the baby can live, if given expert care.

The mother is now conscious of the weight she is carrying. Energetic games or cycling are usually given up by now, but walking, daily exercises and gardening may generally be continued.

At the End of Thirty-two Weeks

The foetus is nearly 16 in (40cm) long and weighs about 3½ lb (1½kg). There is hair on the scalp, but the nails do not reach the tips of the fingers. The size of the uterus is now greatly increased and may cause a little discomfort by its upward pressure.

At the End of Thirty-six Weeks

Length about 17½ in (44cm) and weight about 5½ lb (2½kg). The downy hair on the skin is disappearing though some still remains and the skin is also covered with a fatty substance. At about this stage, the position of the uterus usually changes again, sinking down a little, thus relieving any possible pressure, and the baby's head may sink down into the pelvis if it is a first pregnancy.

At the End of the Fortieth Week

Full Term. Length 19-20 in (49-51cm) and weight about $6\frac{1}{2}$-8 lb ($3-3\frac{1}{2}$kg). The nails are fully grown, and the skin is smooth. The baby is now ready to be born. The head and abdomen of a new baby are relatively big. All the bones are not yet completely ossified, notably the skull, to allow for its moulding during birth.

The date of the baby's probable birth is calculated as 280 days from the first day of the last menstrual period. The birth may take place on the appointed day or as much as a fortnight before or after this date, and the birth weight may also vary considerably but this is quite normal.

10.

The Birth

Birth has, unfortunately, come to be traditionally, but erroneously, accepted as a painful, difficult and even dangerous event, but these ideas are now, hopefully, beginning to be overcome. Two lines of approach to this problem have developed, both aimed at making births less painful for the mother and safer for her and the baby. One is basically medical technology, based on doing things *for* the mother and her baby at, and after the birth, and the other is based on things done *by* the mother herself in advance of the birth during her pregnancy, the aim being to try to promote a natural birth, and not one taken over by doctors (however well-intentioned) and machines.

Things Done for the Mother

There is a lot of discussion about the almost complete 'hospitalization of labour' and why, despite increased use of modern technology, our rates of perinatal mortality and handicap are worse than those of many countries such as Sweden, the Netherlands and Japan.

Medical technology has developed various ways of trying to help mothers, including forceps, anaesthetics, analgesics, epidurals, Caesarean section and, most recently, the chemical induction of labour using oxytocin. This last may be used not only to start contractions coming, but to accelerate them and make them stronger when labour has been allowed to start naturally. Such medical technology seems to be taking us further and further away from natural births. With chemical induction, labour may be started before the baby is actually quite ready to be born and, although induction speeds up labour, it can also make the contractions more painful.

Epidural injections numb the mother's pains, but also interfere with her normal bearing down activities, so much so that these injections can sometimes lead to the need for uterine stimulants or forceps delivery. According to the British Medical Journal (18.8.79): 'Induction for purely social or medical convenience is recognized to be bad practice, and is probably less used now than it was five years ago.' The means used to control and monitor labour means that the mother has to lie down, but doctors are trying to find ways of allowing the mother to be 'ambulant', that is, to 'walk round and find the position she is most comfortable in', as she would if she was having her baby at home and because walking about can help the birth progress. Fortunately, it should still be possible, and most desirable, even with an induced birth, for the maternal 'bonding' to take place.

Wonderful as modern technology is, it tends to give mothers a passive role at the birth, taking over what is essentially her great job. Mothers are designed to be active participants, not passive passengers at the birth of their babies. Ideally, the aim of these measures is to reduce the mother's pains, but not to interfere with the birth processes. They are also intended to be absolutely safe for the baby, but so far no such ideal agent or procedure has been produced, and the baby has sometimes suffered from measures designed to be helpful. Quite marvellous work is done with premature and underweight babies who are born at risk, by the skill of doctors and midwives and in intensive care units. However, sometimes it may seem as though advanced medical technology has gone further than is necessary over apparently ordinary births.

The birth situation was rather nicely expressed by Sir Truby King in 1913 when he said: 'It is wiser to put up a fence at the top of a precipice than to maintain an ambulance at the bottom', and the ante-natal preparations suggested here are all designed to help to erect a good fence at the top of the 'precipice' of infant deaths, while medical technology may be said to represent the ambulance at the bottom, which is, of course, still essential to have in reserve for special cases. It is wise to ask your doctor what sort of ante-natal care is available locally as soon as your pregnancy is confirmed.

Things Done by the Mother to Help Herself

It is not nature, but civilization, which has led to births being both painful and dangerous to so many women, and so it should be possible to reverse this trend by mothers becoming more 'primitive' and doing everything that they can to promote natural childbirth. This is a most rewarding goal to work for, as a natural birth is most beneficial to the baby as well as to the mother.

We need to go one step further back, with a vital creative attempt to change the *beginning* of birth, that is, to start from, or even before, the moment of conception, so as to reduce the number of babies ever being born at risk through being underweight and poorly nourished. The idea is that the mother should be active in carrying out good ante-natal preparation by having the right kinds of foods of the highest nutritional quality and to avoid polluting her body with foods of poor or deficient nutritional quality or by smoking. Also by doing exercises and practising relaxation and trained breathing, etc. the mother can minimize in advance the causes of birth pains and of babies being born at risk through faulty nutrition.

Some mothers have found that taking the special flower product, Vita Florum, has greatly helped them in pregnancy and in promoting an easy, natural birth.

If properly prepared, the mother should be able to be very active during the birth, and not just a passive recipient of even the best medical technology, and ideally there should be little if any need for anaesthetics at a baby's birth. If pains are very severe, a hot sitz bath, taken under the care of the nurse, can bring great relief.

Workers for Natural Births

Dr Alice Stockman must have been one of the first, if not the first, doctor to try to promote the idea of natural and easy births for all women with her book *Tokology* (meaning 'Science of Midwifery') first published in 1893 in America and then in 1911 in this country. This book was a revelation of what women themselves could do to help to promote quick and easy births by eating and living on healthy lines.

She stressed the damage that can be done by even a small

degree of constipation, and advocated the extensive use of wholegrain cereals including rice, and fruits, especially oranges, and vegetables as the best basis for a mother's meals. She quotes Professor Huxley as saying: 'We are fully prepared to believe that the bearing of children *ought* to become as free from danger and debility to the civilized mother as it is to the savage.' She says that 'feast on fruits freely' should be the pregnant woman's motto, with fruit at every meal. Fats and sugars, if taken at all, should only be used in very restricted amounts.

Dr Stockman quotes a number of cases of pain-free, or nearly pain-free births experienced by her patients who followed her dietary recommendations during their pregnancies, and these should encourage other mothers to use the same foods.

Since the early years of this century there has been a growing number of books designed to help mothers to help themselves over childbirth, such as, in 1930, *The Foundation of Motherhood* by Dr Pink.

In the 1930s Dr Grantly Dick Read's book presented a revolutionary idea that a great deal of birth-pains are caused by *fears*; the sequence being, fear – tension – pain and more fear, and he stresses the vital importance of relaxation.

In 1948 *Maternity and Post-Operative Exercises* by Margaret Morris was published.

In 1956 The National Childbirth Trust was formed which supplied much helpful information. The Birth Centre, (see *Useful Addresses*), also supplies much helpful information, including that about Dr Leboyer's work and his film, and also about homoeopathic remedies.

In 1959 Dr Vellay and Dr Lamaze introduced a method called 'Psychoprophylaxis' based on the work of Pavlov which used the idea of conditioning women mentally for labour. Their book *Childbirth Without Pain* has some beautiful photographs of women actually giving birth, and smiling with joy as they watch their own baby being born.

In 1975, Dr Leboyer's lovely book *Birth Without Violence* was published and his film released (see *Further Reading*). In these he turned our attention towards the baby, and developed an approach aimed at giving the baby an easy transition from the womb into our world, with dim lights, quiet and a warm fluid environment, so that birth is not a traumatic and painful experience, but babies are treated gently and with respect. He has photographs, one after an orthodox birth, with the baby held upside down by his feet and screaming, with the doctor and parents smiling because it means that the baby is breathing, and a companion one of a new born baby smiling and contented shortly after being born in the manner of Dr Leboyer's new approach. Mothers who are interested in Dr Leboyer's approach to birth could contact the N.C.T. or the Birth Centre for the latest information about midwives or doctors who are interested in his approach.

Doctors and nurses can teach the young mother that her own actions and mental attitude are the vital things at the birth, and that their job is to co-operate with her and help her as necessary, but not to try to do her job for her. Their normal function is to work through the mother, and they should not supercede her natural job in any way.

Onset of Labour

When labour begins, the young mother, whose body has been preparing for the event throughout pregnancy, may find herself, like a young actress before a first night, suffering from a bit of stage fright, but she will also feel excited and exhilarated. Her preparations will have given her confidence and feelings of joy and of self-reliance, and ready to work with doctor and nurse. She will want to help her baby all she can, and to acquit herself creditably in what is her special job.

Although most births now take place in hospital, the mother should not worry about having drugs, etc. that she may not want. She should not be afraid, when she arrives at hospital in early labour, of telling the nurses or doctor if she does not want drugs unless absolutely necessary, and that she does very much want the baby to be delivered onto her bare abdomen before the cord is cut, etc. New mothers should not feel too intimidated by the hospital atmosphere to say what they want, and the staff will normally want to do what the mother wants, if they know what this is, and provided it is not unsuitable.

The first signs that the baby is on the way are usually some irregular pains in the back, and/or colic-like pains in the abdomen. These may pass unnoticed or unidentified by the young mother, especially if they come early or during sleep.

Position of the Baby

Just before the birth, the baby is normally curled up inside the uterus, with the head bent forward, and the knees bent up, and the arms doubled up in front. It is lying head downwards, with its face to the mother's back. This position is the best one, as it ensures that the smallest diameter of the head will pass through the bony arch and birth canal. It is said to occur in over 96 per cent of births. The baby lies protected in a bag of fluid, encased in membranes, inside the strong muscular uterus.

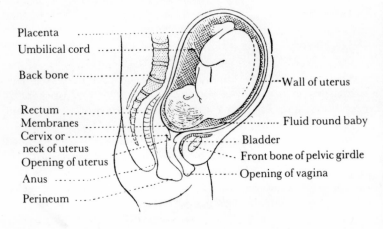

Placenta

Umbilical cord

Back bone

Wall of uterus

Rectum

Membranes

Fluid round baby

Cervix or
neck of uterus

Bladder

Opening of uterus

Front bone of pelvic girdle

Anus

Opening of vagina

Perineum

Figure 2. Diagram of the position of the baby in the uterus. Just before birth, the baby is normally curled up inside the uterus, with head bent forward and knees bent up – as shown here.

'Show'

Sometimes at the time that the birth is expected, the mother will notice that a small piece of slightly blood-stained mucus comes away. This is called the 'show' and it has been present in the mouth of the uterus. The mother's mental attitude at this time is more important than ever before. A feeling of confidence, exhilaration and joy, will help the baby's rapid progress, whereas worry and fear will retard progress and make things painful to the mother.

Three Stages
There are three stages in the birth of a baby.

1. The first stage is dilation of the mouth of the womb.
2. The second stage is expulsion of the baby.
3. The third stage is expulsion of the placenta and embryonic membranes.

The First Stage
Mild, irregular contractions indicate that parturition has started, but even if going to hospital there is normally no need to rush off in a hurry as this stage usually lasts for some hours, though it may be shorter if diet and exercises as preparation for a natural birth have been followed. At hospital, the mother may have a bath, pubic hair may be cut, and she may be given a suppository to empty the bowels. There is no advantage in going to bed at this stage if she is allowed to be up, unless she feels like resting and relaxing.

The mother may be interested to know that the mouth of the uterus has to dilate before the baby can emerge, and the pressure of the fluid in the uterus helps this to take place. The mother may be offered pethidine, but she need not have it if she does not want it. If the mother has practised relaxation daily during her pregnancy these techniques should be a great help at this stage. If the husband has also learnt about his wife's controlled breathing, he can help her by reminding her what she should be doing, and he may also help her by rubbing her back. Most hospitals allow husbands to stay with their wives throughout the birth if they both want this, and this can be a most rewarding experience for them both.

The Second Stage
When the mouth of the uterus is fully dilated, the type of contraction changes. If the waters have not broken naturally

by this stage an amniotomy will be done (this may be done in the first stage, usually to hurry up the contractions or even, at the beginning, to start the labour).

An episiotomy may be done towards the end of the second stage, and is done to prevent the mother 'tearing'. In the old days a good midwife 'guarded the perineum', i.e. prevented a tear without doing an episiotomy: in some hospitals episiotomies are now routine.

Regular contractions of increasing strength take place, and the mother feels a definite urge to help by 'bearing down', that is by muscular activity similar to the work of expelling the faeces. Ideally, the mother now takes a very active part in the birth and the harder she works the better. She may be partially propped up in bed, with pillows, with her knees bent, and may pull on them, or can have a rope or knotted towel attached to the end of the bed to pull on with something to push against with her feet, or she may pull on her husband's hands or arm instead of the rope. It is easier to work to expel the baby in this position than if lying down on one's side, and the husband's arm can be most helpfully encouraging. Another possible position is on hands and knees which is said to be the position instinctively adopted by unattended women.

It is usually during the second half of the second stage of labour that the pains may become really severe, and so it is at this stage that an anaesthetic may be given. This is often of the 'gas and air' type which the mother can hold for herself, and take just as much as she feels she needs to take the edge off the pain, but some mothers do not want any, especially if they have prepared themselves for a natural birth. It is a help to know that the anaesthetic is there should they want it, and no mother should suffer unbearable pain, but it is good when she can remain conscious for the birth and even see her baby emerging, as is possible in the propped up position suggested. Between each contraction, the mother should relax and do her trained breathing.

Bonding
As soon as the head is through the worst of the pains are past,

and then as soon as the baby has fully emerged it is best and natural if he can at once be put onto his mother's abdomen – skin to skin – where she can welcome and caress him and where he can feel her close contact as he did before birth, and so reduce the trauma of his birth for him. This is the very valuable 'bonding' which we know occurs among animals, and is believed to be of great value to both mother and baby in establishing breast-feeding, and in laying the basis for a warm relationship. The separation of the new born baby from his mother at birth is now regarded by many people as damaging and unnecessary. The baby may rootle about to find a nipple and may have a small breast-feed before the cord is severed or he is washed and dressed, and then, if possible, he may be given back to the mother to hold for a while, and perhaps have another little feed before being put into his cot. This further feed helps the third stage of labour.

The Third Stage

After the baby is born there will be more contractions when the placenta and membranes (or afterbirth) are expelled. The doctor or nurse examines this to make sure that none of it has been retained which might cause trouble later. The uterus begins to contract after the birth is completed, and all the parts begin to regain their normal condition. The mother may be washed and made comfortable in bed and may have a warm drink and then relax and rest or sleep.

In some modern hospitals the new-born babies are not now separated away in a nursery, but are kept beside their mothers where they can be fed as wanted, which is much better than separation. Also, any brothers or sisters are generally allowed to see their mother in the ward, and see the new baby, if accompanied by the father or other adult.

Any efforts, such as these, to make the hospital atmosphere more relaxed and homelike, are most welcome, and this is the way modern thinking seems to be moving. Some hospitals are much more ready than others to listen to mothers and try to find out what they want, and to help them to have it when possible, and mothers should continue to try and explain their desires to the doctors and nurses who are attending them, as unless the mother tells them, they cannot be expected to know. Also, mothers' desires may vary, like wanting to have a natural birth, so flexibility by hospital staff is very desirable.

11.

After the Birth

The unit that begun as a partnership has become a family, with new joys and responsibilities, and most modern fathers take a major part in sharing both the joys and work of parenthood.

The Mother

When the mother wakes after her first sleep she may expect a marvellous feeling of peace, joy and fulfilment, and she will be ready for a light and well chosen meal, which should be of a laxative type. It could be soaked and simmered prunes, or apple muesli, with added bran and wheatgerm and milk, followed by 100 per cent wholewheat bread or toast, with butter and honey and a milk drink; or it could be sieved vegetable soup with grated cheese and a little bran, followed by baked apple and yogurt or junket, and a milky drink if liked. The bran is very valuable, because after the birth there may be a tendency for the bowels to be a bit sluggish, and the bran is very valuable in helping to regulate the bowels and because the bran is a valuable source of essential mineral salts and helps in the production of milk.

During the first couple of days, the mother's priorities will be establishing breast-feeding; getting to know her baby and helping him to get to know her. She can begin a few very simple exercises such as tensing and relaxing the muscles of her abdomen and flattening them and then relaxing. She can also tighten and then relax the muscles of her buttocks, and do some daily deep breathing. It is also a good plan to lie flat on her front for about half an hour once or twice a day to help the uterus to maintain its right position. Sometimes expert massage may be given in the first weeks.

Establishing breast-feeding, is dealt with in the next chapter. Her own meals should be regular, even if her baby's may not be at first, and extra drinks, such as vegetable broth, between meals are very valuable. The help and encouragement of the nurse in establishing breast-feeding is invaluable at this stage, as a good start can make all the difference to continued success, and this should be the nurse's joy and satisfaction as well as the mothers.

Nowadays there is no long staying in bed after the birth, and sometimes the mother will probably get up soon after it, possibly to have a bath. Individuals vary, and so does the ease of the birth, so some mothers may need a little more rest than others do. After two weeks the mother should be feeling splendid, but she should not forget that her inside is not yet back to normal, so when home again she should not rush about or take on all the normal household duties, or drive herself too hard, especially if she is breast-feeding her baby.

Doctor's Examination
The doctor will have visited the mother during the first days after the birth, and after three months she should visit him for a final examination. He can then make sure that everything is in order, with nothing present that might lead to trouble in a later pregnancy.

Return of Menstruation
Sometimes menstruation starts again within a few months of the birth even if the mother is breast-feeding, but sometimes it does not restart until after breast-feeding is finished. If it does restart, there is no need to worry or give up the breast-feeding, even though sometimes the baby's digestion may be slightly upset for a day or two, but it quickly settles down.

The Baby
After the mother has had her first meal, the baby may be put to the breast again, sucking from both breasts for a few minutes. The full milk supply does not come immediately, but gradually over the first few days, but the baby should be put to both breasts regularly all the same. This is because the first substance secreted by the breasts, the colostrum is extremely

valuable to him and should be the first substance to enter the stomach, and also because his sucking stimulates the breasts to secrete milk, and most babies have a strong instinct to suck.

Preparations of Vitamins and Mineral Salts

Expectant and nursing mothers should not rely on preparations of mineral salts and vitamins to give them what they need. These should be mainly supplied by a correct choice of the right kinds of good foods. However, it may sometimes be desirable to supplement the best natural diet that the mother can get with some additional natural vitamins or mineral salts such as wheatgerm for the B vitamin complex, vitamin E and iron, and perhaps bone meal tablets for mineral salts. Medicines, apart from such natural supplements, are best avoided and should only be taken when expressly prescribed by the doctor.

Baby's Progress after Birth

Babies vary a little in their development, and boys and girls differ, boys tending to be slightly heavier than girls. The following notes are a general guide to a baby's normal progress. Slight deviation should give no worry at all, but serious deviations suggest the need for expert advice.

Baby at Birth

Weight $7\frac{1}{2}$ lb (3.5kg) approx., length 19-20 in (48-50cm). He is complete in every detail, and the miniature fingers and toes, complete with their tiny nails, are a fresh wonder to every mother. There is hair on the head, but not on the rest of the body, which is, at birth, covered with an oily substance as a protection and to facilitate the birth. The skin is usually pink, but soon fades to a normal flesh colour. There is valuable substance in the baby's stomach, called the meconium, whose function is to establish the regular excretion of the baby's stools in the first week of life. It is dark green in colour. He can sneeze and yawn.

At the End of One Week

The baby will have lost a little weight at first, while adjusting himself to his new way of living, and waiting for the breast milk to come in. He should be able to suckle properly, kick and wave his arms, and stools should be passed – the first few being dark green or nearly black in colour, because of the meconium but later ones should be soft, homogeneous and light yellow. He will like soft light, and will screw up his eyes in bright light. Breast-feeding should be established.

The mother should be feeling well and the milk should have 'come in'. If the pregnancy was well regulated, the birth will have been very little real strain on the mother.

At the End of Two Weeks
He should have regained his birth weight, or even more, and should be feeding well. The mother should not have excessive 'household duties'. It is a good plan for her to have some domestic help at home for at least two weeks more – possibly the father.

At One Month
Dawning of the senses and of attention. The baby enjoys moving objects, people, lights and likes being caressed and being sung to. May raise his head. Likes having a few minutes 'kicking time' on his mother's knee before the evening bath. Provided the mother takes the right foods and has enough water to drink and has a daily rest, she should be able to cope both with some household duties and breast-feeding, with her husband's help.

At Two Months
The baby knows his mother, follows moving lights with his eyes, and can focus both eyes together. Longer kicking times. Responsive smiles.

At Three Months
The baby grips things firmly with his hands. He may be sleeping soundly all night, and regularly in the daytime. The 6 a.m. feed can be given early, if necessary. He enjoys lying on a rug for kicking exercises.

At Four Months
Head can be lifted. The baby plays with his hands, and enjoys

his mother's and father's presence, but may be shy with strangers. He understands approval and disapproval. The baby crows and laughs.

At Five Months
Plays with fingers and toes. Kicks and exercises very strongly. Kicking times, with napkin loosened to allow freedom of movement, before the 10 a.m., 2 p.m., and 6 p.m. feeds. Sieved fruits and vegetables given.

At Six Months
Sometimes the baby has cut his two lower front teeth at this age. He reaches for his toes and handles them, and likes making a noise and banging. Hard-baked crusts for jaw exercises given. May attempt to crawl. One breast-feed sometimes replaced with bottle-feed. Cereals may now be given.

At Seven Months
The baby makes different sounds, and may try to pull himself up. May enjoy a 'Baby Bouncer'.

At Eight Months
The baby is able to sit erect and his responsiveness increases. The quantities of fruit and vegetable purées and other extras should be steadily increasing. The baby may crawl and may be ready to change to three meals a day (omitting the 6 a.m. and 10 p.m. feed) but milk still a valuable part of his meals.

At Nine Months
Crawls vigorously and may pull himself up. The baby can understand a firm but gentle 'No'.

At Ten Months
The baby is very active and makes many new sounds and has a greater variety of foods.

At Eleven Months
The baby may stand with assistance. Gradually less milk is taken and more other foods.

At Twelve Months

May sometimes have six teeth cut, four at the bottom and two at the top. The 'soft spot' in the head is gradually hardening and closing. Says simple words.

As regards the baby's progress, the mother should keep her eyes open for possible upsets, but should not worry unnecessarily. For instance, sometimes a baby will be forward in one respect, but not quite up to average in some other. He may, perhaps, have been teething extensively, and may have an extra lot of teeth, or the weight may be temporarily a little below average, when the mother may sometimes be worrying herself quite unduly.

Weight Gain

After the first fortnight babies normally gain about 8 oz (225g) a week, then from about the fourth month to the sixth month about $1\frac{1}{4}$ lb (550g) a month and from the sixth to twelfth month about 1 lb (450g) a month. At a year the baby generally weighs about 21 lb (9.5kg).

12.

Breast-feeding

Breast-feeding should be regarded as an integral part of having a baby, and not thought of as an optional extra, like taking music at school. Just as an expectant mother should have the right raw materials during her pregnancy for the health of herself and her baby, so should the new born baby himself have the right raw materials for his growth and health, and these materials are provided at their best by good breast milk. To make the highest quality breast milk, it is important for the mother herself to continue to have the best possible quality of food as here advised for her pregnancy.

Colostrum
It is especially important that the first substance that enters the baby's alimentary canal by his mouth should be from his mother's breasts. This is the colostrum, which unique substance is especially designed to prepare the baby's digestive system for its function of digestion, and it also supplies immune bodies which help to guard against infection. If any other substance, such as sugar water, is given before the colostrum, as sometimes happens, then the unique work of the colostrum is impaired, which can only take place normally when it is the *first* food that the baby has.

But breast-feeding is more than just giving the baby the best food for his physical needs, it is also a way of expressing love and joy between mother and baby, so it has tremendous emotional as well as physical value. It is also valuable to the baby as a source of comfort and security and as his first experience of co-operation with another individual for their mutual benefit and happiness.

Rather than just urging mothers to breast-feed their babies, doctors and nurses can greatly help the successful establishment of breast-feeding by creating the right climate for starting it by the procedure of 'bonding'. This procedure should take place if at all possible as it is a most propitious start to successful breast-feeding, but is something of which mothers and babies can all too easily be deprived by too rigid hospital procedures. (See pages 72 and 73.)

With few exceptions, most mothers can breast-feed their babies if they really want to, as breast-feeding is a normal part of the cycle of having a baby, and is one for which mothers have been beautifully and specially designed. So it is worthwhile for mothers to make considerable efforts when necessary to breast-feed their babies. Even if breast-feeding can only be continued for three or four weeks, it is well worth starting breast-feeding and ensuring that the baby does at least get the colostrum in his first feeds. Ideally, however, it should be continued for about the first six months or longer. Sometimes, despite all her efforts, breast-feeding seems unsatisfactory and the mother should not then feel guilty if she has to change to artificial feeding and bottles.

Pre-requisites for Successful Breast-feeding

1. The mother should feel confident and enthusiastic but also relaxed about feeding her baby, realizing that it means that she is giving him his birthright. Thus, breast-feeding should be a joy and service of love. She should have faith in her ability to do this for her baby, and it should take priority over other activities. After all, breast-feeding is more important than brass polishing.

2. She must have the right kind of whole, fresh high quality food and plenty of fluid to produce adequate high quality milk. Adequate rest is also most important as well as sunshine, fresh air and exercise.

3. She should be free from worries and her husband can be a great help when he too realizes the importance of breast-feeding.

4. If there should be any initial difficulties, the mother

should persevere, and the nurses at hospital, and then the District Nurse or Health Visitor, can be a great help, and the mother should not be discouraged by those who do not believe in breast-feeding. National Childbirth Trust Counsellors can be a very great help here.

5. She should realize that when a baby is being successfully breast-fed, he is being nourished with the maximum of efficiency with the minimum of effort.

Special Advantages for the Baby of Good Breast-feeding

1. It helps the development of good jaws and good teeth, with reduced dental decay.

2. Breast milk is easier to digest than are artificial milk mixtures and it gives a good natural growth rate. It also has a better health record than bottle-feeding has, and breast-fed babies are usually noticeably lively and happy looking.

3. Good breast-feeding is still safer than bottle feeding is, although artificial feeding is much safer than it used to be.

4. Some authorities consider that breast-feeding reduces the chances of cot deaths.

5. The loving contact of cuddling by his mother is of great psychological and emotional value to the baby.

6. It gives the new baby a sense of security, and is thought to help the baby to be confident and independent later on.

Special Advantages for the Mother of Breast-feeding

1. It helps her figure return to normal, as sucking at the breasts stimulates the contractions of the uterus.

2. For many women breast-feeding is a deep joy and helps to develop a strong emotional bond between the mother and her baby.

3. It contributes to the mother's peace of mind by her

knowing that she is giving her baby the best possible food.

4. Breast-feeding is quicker, and cheaper than bottle feeding is, and when once satisfactorily established it is also much easier, as there is no measuring, sterilizing or warming up to be done, and it is always ready, which is especially valuable in the early days when feeding 'on demand', or if it is needed for night feeding.

Comparison of Breast Milk with Cow's Milk

We should remember that breast milk is designed for babies and cow's milk for cows so that there are definite differences in the chemical composition of breast milk and cow's milk. Cow's milk contains more protein than breast milk does, and much more of the less easily digested protein casein than of the protein albumen. Also cow's milk contains more mineral salts, particularly much more sodium, calcium, potassium, and magnesium than breast milk does, which makes it unsuitable for babies without much modification, and it is not yet possible to modify cow's milk so as to make a perfect substitute for breast milk.

Table 1. Percentage Content of Nutrients in Breast Milk and Cow's Milk

Nutrient		Breast Milk		Cow's Milk	
Protein {	Casein	0.8	} 2.01	2.88	} 3.39
	Albumen	1.21		0.51	
Fat		3.74		3.68	
Sugar		6.37		4.94	
Ash		0.30		0.72	

Cow's milk has first to be diluted to bring the protein concentration nearer to that of breast milk. It must then have milk sugar and a little fat added to bring these up again to be closer to breast milk. Also the mineral salts have to be adjusted. Breast milk also has certain protective immunizing bodies in it, and 'buffer substances' to help in the digestion of the casein which are lacking in cow's milk.

Establishing Lactation

Sir Truby King, the famous New Zealand doctor, did a great deal of valuable work in promoting breast-feeding and showing the need for it, but unfortunately he also believed in 'feeding by the clock' and sticking to a four-hourly feeding regime with no night feeding. This is now no longer considered at all desirable.

Fortunately for both mothers and babies the days are gone when it was considered necessary to 'feed by the clock', either as to the length or frequency of feeds. Thus, worried and anxious mothers no longer have to listen miserably to their baby crying, not daring to feed him because it is not yet four hours after the last one. After the birth, changes will be taking place in the mother's glandular system to inaugurate the secretion of milk, and the first fluid secreted will be the precious colostrum.

Though the milk does not normally 'come in' fully for the first three days, the feeding in these days is very important for establishing good breast-feeding, and for ensuring that the baby gets all the colostrum. Since sucking stimulates the breasts to secrete milk, it is generally a mistake to give the baby a bottle-feed as he is then unlikely to suck so hard at the breast, so stimulation is reduced. Occasionally even one bottle-feed may be enough to create an allergy.

By the third day when the milk has come in plentifully, care may sometimes be needed to see that the baby is not over-fed, as his needs are still relatively small, so it is important not to feed him too much, but of course he must have enough. One result of over-feeding in the early days is that the baby may cry through having indigestion. This may make the mother fear that her milk does not suit him, when really he is just having a little too much. This can generally be adjusted to suit the baby's actual requirements.

Feeding on Demand

Instead of feeding by the clock, mothers are now allowed to feed 'on demand', which means that the baby is fed whenever he is hungry and cries for a feed, perhaps every 1½-2 hours at first, and this frequent stimulation of the breasts can increase the quantity of milk produced, so that the baby may then get more milk at each feeding period and so should gradually want feeds less frequently, and may develop a regular rhythm.

Regular Rhythm of Feeding Times

Some babies may adopt a regular rhythm of four-hourly feeding of their own accord almost from the start, which is very convenient, but others may need more frequent feeds for a while. However, by about three months a regular rhythm of four-hourly feeding can usually be established, having feeds at approximately 6 a.m., 10 a.m., 2 p.m., 6 p.m., and 10 p.m.

Frequent Feeds

Just occasionally a baby may be very wakeful and may cry so much that his feeds 'on demand' may become so frequent that neither he or his mother get enough sleep. Probably he can be helped here if his mother tries to make the feeds a little longer so that he gets more milk at a time, and also gets the richer milk that comes later in the feed. In this way he may well be better satisfied and so not want a feed quite so often. Also, he may just need the comfort of contact with his mother, and so carrying him about in his carrying sling after a feed for a short time, while his mother gets on with jobs, before putting him gently into his warmed cot, may be the answer.

Another aid to a sleepless baby could be the use of a Winganna fleece. These lambswool fleeces for babies have a reputation for providing babies with a sound and restful sleep. Information can be obtained from Sandy Hill Enterprises, (see Useful Addresses).

Babies vary a lot, even in the same family, some being very good sleepers and some others being very wakeful, and refusing to be settled to sleep in their cot after a feed.

Infrequent Feeds

Sometimes a small baby may go to the other extreme, and may not wake to demand a feed often enough, when the mother may have to rouse him gently and get him properly awake before putting him to the breast. If not getting enough breast milk, he may not be lively enough to demand a feed, and may suffer from malnutrition, even though the mother thinks that because he appears to be sleeping well everything is alright. It is essential for small babies to be weighed at the clinic each week, so that the nurse can check their progress and advise the mother if the baby is putting on too much weight or not enough, and what to do if anything is needed. Do not let the baby go for over four hours between daytime feeds in the first months.

While her baby is not a little automaton, to be fed by the clock, neither does his mother want to turn him into a little tyrant wanting to be fed all the time. She has to develop a happy medium.

Crying

The baby's only method of expressing his disapproval of things is to cry. He may cry because he is hungry, but he may also cry because he is thirsty, or has wind or has been over-fed and has indigestion, or because he is too hot or has a wet and uncomfortable nappy or because he has a tickling vest or is in an uncomfortable position or, of course, because he is lonely and wants his mother. The mother has to try to interpret what he is crying about, and should not think it is always, necessarily, hunger. Persistent crying indicates that all is not quite right, and every effort has to be made to try to find out what is wrong, and make suitable adjustments. Sometimes, it could mean that the baby might do better on bottle-feeding, but there can be wind and colic with bottle-feeding too.

Forming Good Habits

The gentle training entailed in developing a bit of rhythm over meals, sleep, bath and bed should not hurt the baby, if wisely done, and it can be beneficial as the baby's first experience of a regular behaviour pattern. What is more, such training can help mothers to have a reasonably organized life.

Improving the Milk Supply

If the baby is found to be not gaining enough weight, or if he cries a lot, it could mean that he needs longer or more frequent feeds, or that the mother's milk supply needs improving through her diet, with possibly a little more protein – and possibly a little more 100 per cent wholewheat bread and butter. She might have an egg beaten up in milk or orange juice at 11 a.m. or a drink of Complan at bedtime. Extra vitamin B may also help to improve the supply.

She will also probably need to take a little more fluid and some mothers find that it helps to have a glass of water during each feeding period. Halfway through each feed and again at the end of a feed, the mother should hold the baby up against her shoulder and gently rub his back upwards to help him to bring up his wind. This is because some air is generally swallowed with the milk, and this can interfere with further feeding. To increase her milk supply, the mother should also have more rest. She can also stimulate the breasts by alternate hot and cold bathing after a morning and afternoon feed.

Tired Mother

If the mother has not only her household duties, but possibly one or more other children to care for, she may find life very difficult and become very tired. Breast-feeding may suffer. Here the help of the father is invaluable and can make all the difference between being able to continue breast-feeding and giving it up. It will also help her to feed the baby lying down on her bed. Even if not breast-feeding, the father's help will still be valuable, but if this is not possible, because of his job, then some other help will be very desirable for a little time until the mother is used to her busy life, and the baby is a little older.

A drink of brose, the 'tired shepherd's drink', and a rest of ten to fifteen minutes is wonderfully refreshing for a tired mother.

Possibility of Four Feeds a Day

Sometimes the mother's milk is very good and plentiful, with more than enough to satisfy her baby, so that he may sleep regularly over the feeding times and gain a lot of weight. This may indicate that four feeds in the 24 hours would be better than five, and sometimes quite small babies may sleep soundly through the 10 p.m. feed until 5 or 6 a.m. so that the 10 p.m. feed may be omitted, if the baby continues to sleep well and gain weight. Usually this does not happen until the baby is about seven months old but if it does happen earlier it can be a perfectly satisfactory arrangement. Alternatively, four feeds may be given at five hourly intervals, say, 7 a.m., 12 noon, 5 p.m. and 10 p.m. with possibly a drink of 2-4 fl. oz (50-100ml) cooled boiled water, possibly flavoured with a little orange juice at about 3 p.m. if he is awake. This will give him the additional *fluid* he may perhaps need, even though he is getting adequate food from the breast.

Suggested Diet and Regime for a Nursing Mother

To feed her baby satisfactorily and keep her own health and good looks, it is essential that a nursing mother should look after her own health.

Food

1. Continue to have the right kinds of whole, fresh, natural foods – dairy produce and other protein foods, wholegrain cereals (particularly 100 per cent wholewheat bread), fresh and dried fruits, salads and cooked vegetables, including potatoes baked in their skin, if possible. She will probably find that her appetite has increased, which is natural, so she may need a little more protein and, perhaps, more dried fruit and potatoes, but she does not want to over-eat.

2. As far as possible, avoid the deficiency foods white flour and white sugar and all the many foods and drinks and sweets, etc. made with them.

3. It is cheaper and more sensible to buy some 'extras' such as an extra egg, wheatgerm, fruit, honey or nuts for the mother, rather than to wean the baby and buy proprietary foods for him.

Fluid

1. The mother should take extra drinks during the day between meals (such as vegetable broth, honey tea, or brose.)

2. Drinking a glass of water during each feeding period is
   helpful to many mothers.

Bowels

Maintain a soft daily bowel evacuation, taking a little
unprocessed bran to ensure this if necessary.

Smoking

Mothers should not smoke when breast-feeding.

Sunshine, Fresh Air and Exercise

Deep breathing, sun and air bathing and daily adequate
exercise should all be included as routine during breast-
feeding, as they contribute greatly towards keeping up the
supply of good breast milk and to the mother's own good
health. Circulatory exercises for the arms, neck and shoulders
assist the flow, and strengthen the supporting breast muscles.

Rest

Cows have a very placid existence which helps their milk
production, and similarly a mother benefits from a calm and
placid existence if she is to produce good milk. This is not
always easy, but the mother needs a good night's rest and
generally in the early days, a daily rest on her bed after the 2
p.m. feed. If she becomes too overtired it will affect her milk
supply adversely. If her duties make a rest seem quite
impossible and she feels a little tired, she should make a
practice of feeding her baby lying down on her bed. If she has
a toddler as well as a baby she may be able to take a rest
whenever he has his daily rest.

Failure to supply the system with these essentials is one
reason why some mothers feel 'run down' and tired when
breast-feeding, but this should not happen if the mother does
follow the above elementary suggestions.

Possible Difficulties over Breast-feeding

While it is true that breast-feeding is a natural job, it does
sometimes happen that minor difficulties may arise.
Generally, however, these are easily put right, and should not
lead the mother to think that she cannot feed her baby

satisfactorily. She can discuss them with an N.C.T. counsellor, and get very helpful advice.

Sometimes the baby may be very sleepy and refuse to suck properly, in which case he should be gently but completely roused for a few minutes before the feed, and given several opportunities to bring up any wind. He may also gulp the food too quickly, possibly giving himself indigestion, when the mother should restrict the flow of milk a little by putting her first and second finger each side of the nipple in a 'V', so controlling the flow for a little while.

Again, if the mother is anxious, or is not looking after her own diet properly, or not having enough rest, breast-feeding may suffer, but these things can usually be put right, if the mother takes stock of herself.

Night Feeding

The new born baby will almost always need a feed in the night. At first he cannot be expected to sleep through the night and will probably wake for a feed between 2.0 and 3.0 a.m. if not before. When the baby is taking larger meals in the daytime and is gaining weight satisfactorily, he will very often give up the night time feeds himself.

If he does not do this by three months, but is gaining weight satisfactorily, he may be helped by being given a small drink of cooled, boiled water instead. The baby may cry for the feed a few times but can just be given water, changed if necessary and turned over and made comfortable, and should soon, in this way, be helped to learn to sleep through the night. The first feed of the day may be given earlier than usual if the baby wakes and is hungry. After it he will then generally sleep well, though some babies are just wakeful, irrespective of feeding needs. When night feeding, it is a help to have the baby's cot right beside the mother's bed, so that she can just lean over and pick him up when he wakes and cries, and then feed him cuddled up in bed with her. When a night feed is no longer given, and the baby sleeps through the night, it is generally best for the baby to sleep in a separate room.

How to Tell if All is Well

If the baby is gaining weight satisfactorily, the stools are normal (soft and yellow) and the baby is contented and generally sleeps well, then the mother can feel that all is well.

Drinks of Water for Baby

Sometimes a baby may be thirsty but not in need of a feed, i.e. milk. Drinks of cooled boiled, unsweetened water may then be given from a small bottle. In hot weather, or if the baby is worried with his teeth, such drinks may be helpful.

Mothering

Play and mothering are as essential for a baby's health and happiness as is food and sleep even when the baby is quite tiny. Beginning with about ten minutes before one or two feeds, the length and frequency of play times should be gradually increased as the baby grows older. The late afternoon before bath time is a good time for play and mothering, including talking to the baby, who enjoys his mother's voice, even when he does not know what she is saying.

13.

Introduction of New Foods

Good breast milk is the most perfectly constituted food that a baby can have, and the first foods other than breast milk that a baby is given should be of the highest nutritional quality too. This means that white sugar and white flour products are best avoided.

Weaning consists in teaching the baby to take the right foods other than breast milk from some source other than the breast, and to take it by some means other than sucking. Weaning is also used to mean substituting a modified milk mixture for breast milk. If the mother is in good health and the baby gaining weight satisfactorily, the mother may often continue breast-feeding for eight months or longer, but usually sometime between six and eight months it may be considered advisable to begin to substitute some breast-feeds with a milk-feed from a teacher beaker. However, before this the baby should already have become accustomed to taking some 'extras' such as diluted fruit and vegetable juices and sieved fruit and vegetable *purées* and to chewing baked crusts.

Introduction of Juices
The secret of success is to introduce all new foods in very small amounts one at a time to start with and to increase them gradually, so that they become accepted as a normal part of meals. Orange juice to start with is valuable because it supplies vitamin C and iron, and is usually enjoyed by the baby beginning with half a teaspoonful freshly-pressed and strained juice in two teaspoonsful of cooled, boiled water. Other juices can then be introduced, followed by fruit and vegetable *purées*. Babies should not be given baby cereals before about six months because until this age, they will

generally not have developed the digestive juices needed to deal with cereals properly. If given too early they can lead to indigestion or allergies. The first cereals can well be fingers of baked crusts to chew at. Starch in the form of sieved potato and sieved banana can be given earlier.

Though a breast-fed baby has less need of orange juice than a bottle-fed baby, it is still a good plan to give the breast-fed baby orange juice too, and it is most easily given from a small bottle. A good time is between 4.30 and 5 p.m. when the baby is usually awake and ready for a drink and playtime. Alternatively, it can be given between 9.00 and 9.30 a.m. and as the amount taken increases, half may be given in the morning and the rest in the evening.

Other diluted raw juices are also good, such as tangerine, apple, grape, prune or carrot juice, and variety is good.

Guidelines for Giving Raw Juices

1. The juice should be freshly prepared and strained.
2. Sugar should not be added.
3. The juice must be suitably diluted with cooled, boiled water and can be tried from about one month.
4. Preferably, it should be given half to one hour before the next breast feed, but such timing may sometimes be a little difficult, if feeding on demand.
5. Preferably, it should be given about two hours after the previous breast-feed.
6. The baby should not be wakened to give him juices.
7. Each new juice should be begun as half a teaspoonful only, and suitably diluted, but the amount can be increased fairly quickly.
8. Very acid juices, such as strawberry or plum, are best not used.
9. If orange juice does not seem to suit the baby, tangerine or apple or grape juice can be tried.

Introduction of Fruit and Vegetable Purées
Between three and five months, babies can start to have 'tastes' of sieved vegetables or fruits, but babies vary and some

may not want any at four months. If they do not, the mother should not bother about these feeds. When the breast milk is good, and the baby is thriving, such extras may not be needed until the baby is about six months old, but having them can be interesting educationally for the baby, if he likes them.

Purées can be bought in little jars or tins or as dry powders, all specially prepared for babies. When starting with very small amounts, the powdered kinds may be more convenient, but as the baby takes larger amounts, the jars will no longer be wasteful. Mothers can decide for themselves which suit their own baby best. *Purées* can also be made at home, using fresh fruit or vegetables. Carrots, spinach, swedes, sprouts, tomatoes, apples, prunes can all be used. *Purées* can have a laxative effect, so care must be taken not to overdo them, by giving too much too soon.

Different from the juices, sieved fruits or vegetables should be given as part of a breast-feed, either at the beginning or the end depending on the baby's hunger for his breast-feed. Initially, they are given during just one feed, say the 2 p.m. feed but, later, they can be given before the 10 a.m. or 6 p.m. feeds too and, later still, before all three of these feeds if liked.

Guidelines for the Introduction of Sieved Fruits and Vegetables

1. If *purées* are made at home, vegetables should be conservatively cooked in a minimum of water, for the shortest time needed, without salt or soda added, and then sieved.
2. Raw fruits should have skins and seeds removed and be sieved or finely grated.
3. Give half a teaspoonful only of each new item to start with, just one at a time, increasing the amount gradually as the baby gets used to it.
4. No forcing or excessive pressure should be used, and if one particular item is refused it should be omitted for a few days.
5. Variety of fruits and vegetables is valuable.
6. When first giving sieved foods, the baby should be

comfortably held on his mother's knee, and just a 'taste' of the food should be put on the tip of the spoon, not the whole half a teaspoonful at once. Soon the baby can sit up in his chair for these foods.

7. When the baby shows a desire to try to 'help' with using a spoon to feed himself, this may be encouraged, even if it is a bit messy, but there is no advantage in trying to hurry this activity if the baby is not ready for it.

Suggestions for Introducing 'Extras' to Babies

The introduction of 'extras' has here been given in stages from one to ten months, with approximate ages given, but each baby must be treated as an individual, and these ages are just a guide as to general averages only, and are not meant to be a programme to be strictly followed. Some babies may be expected to progress more quickly than others, and some more slowly, but both can be perfectly satisfactory. These extras are of course, supplementary to the regular breast or bottle feeds.

One to Three Months

Half a teaspoonful freshly-pressed and strained orange juice in two teaspoonsful cooled, boiled water, increasing to two teaspoonsful orange juice in four teaspoonsful cooled, boiled water. The amount of diluted juice given can be further increased if desired, and one juice drink can be given at about 9.30 a.m. and a different one at 4.30 p.m. from about three months. Often first given between 4 and 5 p.m. when the baby is awake and sociable. Half may be given in the morning if liked, as the baby takes more and other juices such as grape or apple or tangerine juice may be tried as alternatives.

At about three months half a teaspoonful of freshly-pressed raw carrot juice may be given with the midday feed.

Three to Four Months

Juices as before, but quantities may be increased. At 2 p.m. half a teaspoonful sieved steamed carrots, increasing gradually to three teaspoonsful may be given. At about 4.30 p.m. drink of diluted orange juice may be offered.

Five Months

Juices as before.

10 a.m.   Half teaspoonful sieved baked apple, before, during or after milk feed, increasing gradually.

2 p.m.   As for four months. Quantities may be increased if wanted, and other vegetables introduced.

1 teaspoonful sieved old potato may be given with the vegetable.

4.30 p.m.   After a juice drink, a hard-baked finger of wholewheat bread can occasionally be held by the mother for the baby to chew at.

6 p.m.   Half a teaspoonful sieved ripe banana in two teaspoonsful milk mixture.

Six Months (*may be on four milk feeds a day*)

Juices as before.

10 a.m.   As in previous stage, and half a teaspoonful sieved avocado pear can also be tried.

2 p.m.   Other extras that can be introduced one at a time are: a quarter teaspoonful egg yolk, a quarter teaspoonful curd cheese, a quarter teaspoonful sieved pulse food (lentils). Egg should be given no more than twice a week at this age.

4.30 p.m.   As in previous stage. Baked crust to chew can be given regularly.

6 p.m.   Add half a teaspoonful Baby Familia (baby muesli) to two teaspoonsful sieved ripe banana and milk, and later add a quarter teaspoonful Bemax. A taste of Marmite can be put on the baked finger of bread, and later a taste of honey. This can be offered to the baby at the 10 a.m. feed, and/ or the 2 p.m. feed. Instead of baked bread, a piece of peeled, raw apple, or a well scrubbed piece of raw carrot may be held, taking care that baby does not take large pieces and choke.

Cow's milk, pasteurized, can be given after eight months. It need not be boiled, but should be used straight from a well-shaken bottle and have boiling water, at the rate of one quarter boiling water to three-quarters milk, added to it to take the chill off it, and slightly dilute it at first. It can generally be taken undiluted by eleven to twelve months.

Seven to Eight Months

Meals follow the same pattern as before, but with increased quantities and a wider variety of fruits and vegetables. May change to three meals a day omitting both the 6 a.m. and 10 p.m. feeds, but this change should not be rushed. Feeding pattern might then be as follows:

On waking.   Drink of diluted orange juice.

8 a.m.   One to three teaspoonsful baby muesli in a little milk, with sieved baked apple or grated raw apple and a quarter teaspoonful Bemax.
Baked crust to chew at.
Breast or diluted milk from cup or beaker.

10.30 a.m.   Drink of diluted fruit juice followed by sleep in pram.

12.30 p.m.   One to two tablespoonsful sieved vegetables with one to two teaspoonsful sieved or very well mashed baked potato with a half to one teaspoonful egg yolk, or one to two teaspoonsful curd cheese or sieved pulse food.
Breast or diluted cow's milk from a small cup or teacher beaker.
Crust to chew at.

4.00 p.m.   Drink of diluted fruit juice.

4.30-   One to two teaspoonsful freshly-pressed, raw
  5.00 p.m.   carrot juice, may be given here or at a 2 p.m. feed.
Two to three teaspoonsful baby muesli with a little milk and some sieved or well mashed ripe banana.
One or two fingers of bread and butter with a taste of honey or Marmite. Baked crust to chew at.
Breast or diluted cow's milk from cup or feeder.

10-   Breast or milk feed if wanted. (Possibly a small
  10.30 p.m. feed only).

Nine to Ten Months

On waking.   Diluted orange juice.

8 a.m.	Fruit and baby muesli at breakfast can be increased and the fruits varied, and the use of a cup or feeder for the milk drink will probably become regular.
	Toast and butter and a taste of honey can follow the muesli.
10.30 a.m.	Drink of diluted fruit juice followed by sleep in pram.
12.30 p.m.	As for previous months, increasing and varying foods as desired. A second course of junket or yogurt or baked custard with a little fruit (sieved prunes or baked apple or sieved or grated fresh fruit) if the baby likes this. The milk feed may be slightly reduced.
4 p.m.	Drink of diluted fruit juice may be given and something to chew on.
5 p.m.	A toast sandwich of finely chopped lettuce and a little cream cheese or Marmite, or tomato sandwich could be introduced for a change.
	Milk to drink.
10 p.m.	May drop the 10 p.m. feed, but can still have it if wanted.

As the non-milk part of the meals increases, the amount of milk taken may gradually decrease, but for most babies milk is still a valuable part of their meals.

Enjoyment of 'Extras'
These extras are meant to be enjoyed by the baby, and as with older children, meals should be fun, and the baby should not be petted or coerced to eat. He should eat because he himself enjoys his food, rather than to please his mother.

Baked Bread Fingers to Chew
A healthy baby is always testing things by putting them in his mouth and he loves biting and chewing. Baked crusts are given both to help the jaws and teeth to develop properly and to help to teach the baby that foods are for chewing. The time from six months to two years is most important for learning this lesson, as if not encouraged the instinct to chew food may wane.

Vegetable Broth

As a change from raw juices or as an additional drink or as a substitute for some of the milk in hot weather or if the baby is teething, drinks of clear vegetable broth can be taken with advantage. A taste of Marmite or some other vegetable extract can be added for flavouring. Home-made vegetable broth can be a good source of vitamins and mineral salts.

Meat and Meat Products

Contrary to what some people believe, meat is not necessary before a year, and some authorities consider that it is best deferred until the baby is at least two years old. All the necessary protein, B vitamins, and iron can be obtained from such foods as 100% wholewheat bread, milk, cheese, yogurt, eggs, pulse foods including soya products, and nuts and vegetables. Many babies do not like meat.

Deficiency Foods

As well as seeing that babies have the highest quality foods, care should also be taken to see that as far as conceivably possible they do *not* have the two major deficiency foods of civilization, white flour and white sugar, but have wholegrain cereals and natural sugars in their place.

Babies should be protected from acquiring a taste for white sugar by not being given sweets and fancy foods made with white sugar.

14.

Weaning and Bottle-feeding

Ideally, the replacement of the breast-feeding with bottle-feeding should not take place before the baby is about six months old, when it may not be necessary to use a bottle at all. Sometimes, however, if the mother has other small children and little help in the house, she may find it too exhausting to breast-feed for so long. If she does, she should not worry, as every week of successful breast-feeding she has done will have been invaluable. It may not be sensible to continue to try to breast-feed if she is very tired and the baby is not thriving, in which case it will be better for both mother and baby to start to replace the breast-feeds. Since sometimes an emergency may arise, it is as well to be prepared for this possibility and to know something about bottle-feeds.

When it has been decided to start to wean, the usual pattern is to give one bottle-feed a day, in place of the breast-feed at 10 a.m. for a week, and the following week two bottle-feeds a day usually at 10 a.m. and 6 p.m., continuing with any extras as already indicated. The following week the 2 p.m. feed can also be replaced, and then the 6 a.m. feed. If liked, the 10 p.m. breast-feed (or alternatively the 6 a.m. breast-feed) may be continued for a little longer. If there is plenty of milk for one of these feeds, it can be a good idea to continue with it, especially if the weaning was begun early.

Types of Modified Milks

There are various milk mixtures now available which have been modified from cow's milk to make them as near breast milk in their composition as possible, having a considerably reduced mineral salt content. Two such milk products for the artificial feeding of babies are:

1. Cow and Gate Premium
2. S.M.A. Gold Cap

They should be made up accurately according to the instructions given, and given in the amounts suggested, for the baby's age and weight. As a general guide a baby needs $2\frac{1}{4}$-$2\frac{1}{2}$ oz milk mixture per pound of body weight in 24 hours e.g. a 12 lb baby might be expected to need 12 x $2\frac{1}{2}$ oz of milk mixture, i.e. 30 oz or five feeds of 6 oz each. So, if just one feed is being given, it would be expected to be a 6 oz feed. This is a guide only, and should not be rigidly enforced, but it is important not to over-feed the baby in the first few feeds of bottle-feeding. Premature attempts to make the baby give up sucking when he gives up the breast, and not to give him a bottle at all, are not really necessary and can create needless emotional distress.

If the baby sometimes does not want to finish a bottle, he should not be pressed to do so, but if this happens repeatedly the mother should re-check what she is giving him. Later, when the baby is a bit older the bottle can usually be omitted without difficulty. Fruit juices can sometimes be taken from a teacher beaker from about six to seven months instead of from a small bottle. Whole, unmodified cow's milk can usually be drunk at eleven to twelve months, (some authorities allow it well before this) but a few teaspoonsful can be taken before this with fruit or muesli.

Giving the First Bottle

Some babies take to the bottle easily, but others may be difficult. At first the milk should come easily to the baby, and a three-holed teat is a good type to use, or the hole in any teat can be enlarged if necessary. Any teat can be softened by soaking in water before use. The milk mixture should be accurately prepared and put into the bottle which should then be placed in a jug of hot water, if necessary, to warm up to blood heat. The mother can make sure it is the right temperature by shaking a few drops onto the back of her wrist before giving it to the baby.

The baby should always be comfortably nursed when having his bottle, partly because he still needs the close and happy contact with his mother, and partly because, unless the bottle is held, the baby cannot get a proper pull at it. If he is just propped up in his pram, the bottle may slip out of place and he may start to suck air instead of milk. He also needs to be held up to break the wind halfway through and at the end of the bottle-feed as with breast-feeding.

Refusal of the Bottle

In extreme cases, if the baby persistently refuses to suck the bottle, it may help if someone other than the mother, perhaps the father, gives the first few bottles, as the baby may associate his mother too closely with the breast, and her arms and presence may encourage him to demand the breast at all costs. In such cases it may help to give the first bottle at 10 p.m. when the baby is sleepy, or at 6 a.m. when he is quite hungry, but the mother should not give the breast instead of the rejected bottle. The baby may get enough from four feeds, in which case the bottle should be given in place of another feed as well.

Alternatively, sometimes a teacher beaker may be tried, successfully.

Early Bottle-Feeding

After reading the chapter on breast-feeding, a mother will realize how important and valuable breast-feeding is for her baby, especially in the first month, when the baby already has many adjustments to make. If artificial feeding is necessary in the first month, the baby will probably be under the care of a nurse or doctor, who will then supervise the feeding to some extent.

In general, bottle-feeding before four months is undesirable, and should be avoided, if at all possible. However, if for some reason breast-feeding really cannot be managed, the mother should not feel guilty, but should do everything she can to make the bottle-feeding as good as it can be, which, in these days, can be very good indeed. She should choose a good modified cow's milk product and make it up according to the instructions on the tin for her baby's age, though the first few bottles may be best made up just a little weaker than this, especially if her baby is underweight, when a slightly weaker mixture may be desirable at first.

The same routine for bottle-feeding as for breast-feeding is generally the best plan, i.e. five feeds at four-hourly intervals, but with a very small baby, say under seven pounds, six feeds may be better. The baby should not be overfed.

With bottle-feeding it seems that it is easier to establish a regular routine of four-hourly feeding than it sometimes is with breast-feeding, so this should be done if possible.

Additions of Fruit and Vegetable Juices and Purées

The fruit and vegetable juices and *purées* suggested for breast-fed babies are even more important for bottle-fed babies.

One reason for modifying cow's milk for young babies is that it contains much more of the mineral salts, particularly sodium and potassium, than breast milk does, and an excess of these can be bad for the baby's kidneys, so they have to be reduced. The difference is understandable, as breast milk is designed for babies, while cow's milk is designed for calves, who have a different growth rate.

Intolerance of Cow's Milk

Occasionally a baby may be found to have an intolerance of cow's milk, in which case suitably modified goats' milk may be acceptable, or the baby may be given a good plant milk, such as Plamil, on which babies generally do very well. This plant milk can be very useful if the baby or child suffers from eczema or colds or catarrh, as these troubles are often aggravated by cow's milk.

Additions of Vitamins

Some addition of vitamins, particularly A and D, are generally desirable, especially in the winter months, and the Department of Health supplies vitamin drops specially for babies. These additions should not be overdone.

Vitamin D

A good source of vitamin D is the effect of sunshine and fresh air on the baby's skin, but when this is not possible, some supplement of this vitamin and vitamin A may be desirable, especially in the winter. Good foods are a natural source of vitamins e.g. butter and eggs supply some vitamins A and D.

Vitamin B Complex

The B vitamin complex may be supplemented with wheatgerm (Bemax or Froment) but should also always be supplied by wholewheat bread as a matter of course.

Vitamin C

Vitamin C should be adequately supplied by fresh raw fruit and vegetable juices, but actually it is also included in the D.H.S.S. recommended drops.

Care of Bottles and Teats

All bottles and teats must be kept scrupulously clean. After use they should be rinsed out with cold water and then washed with a bottle brush in hot soapy water, sterilized, rinsed and scalded and left to drain. Several bottles should be available. Teats should be washed immediately after use, turned inside out and rubbed with salt, sterilized and rinsed and kept covered until wanted again. Sterilizing tablets can be used.

It can save time and trouble to use Playtex Disposable Bottles, and sometimes these bottles appear to reduce the amount of air swallowed by the babies. If a little too expensive for regular use, these bottles can be very helpful on holidays or if the mother is very busy.

Use of a Dummy

There is considerable difference between the energetic sucking of the teat of a bottle to draw milk, for a short time at specified times a day, and the relaxed and prolonged sucking at a dummy, with no exertion. The continued presence of a dummy in the baby's mouth can push the soft palate up and push the developing teeth outwards, and can tend to promote mouth breathing. There may be occasions with a sick baby when a dummy can be used, but its regular use by a healthy and properly cared for baby should be regarded as undesirable and unnecessary. If used, it must be kept clean by regular washing.

QUANTITIES OF MILK USED

As a rough guide, babies will need 2½ oz (70 ml) milk mixture per pound of body weight, up to 40 oz (11.4 dl). On this calculation a baby of 12 pounds (5.4 kg) would take 30 oz (8.5 dl) of milk mixture, that is five feeds of 6 oz (1.7 dl) each, and a baby of 16 pounds (7.25 kg) (at 6 months) would take 40 oz (1.14 dl) or five feeds of 8 oz (2.3 dl) each in the 24 hours. These are not hard and fast rules, but a general guide, but 40 oz (11.4 dl) of milk mixture should be accepted as the maximum. At the age of six months, babies are normally having some other foods in small amounts, and these will gradually be increased, so that there should be no need for an increase in the amount of milk taken, and in fact the amount of milk tends to decrease as the baby takes more of the other foods.

The composition of the milk mixture will also change, so that by one year, the baby may be taking whole unsweetened milk, in three meals a day, having usually 1 – 1¼ (0.51) pints of milk a day. However, babies vary, so hard and fast rules are not desirable, and the milk may continue to be slightly diluted even at one year.

15.

Routine and Management of Baby

A new-born baby has a tremendous lot to learn. He must adapt himself to a new environment and use his lungs to breath, to adjust to light and noise and to the sensations of being bathed and handled. He also has to learn to take his food by sucking instead of from his mother's blood stream. To help him he should have gentle handling with loving contact with his mother, and the comfort of breast-feeding.

Regular Feeding Times
The gradual establishment of a routine of feeding can be very beneficial, and is a useful piece of subconscious training.

Apart from feeding times, the new-born baby's routine includes a bath and a change of clothes at about 9.30 a.m. and having the face and buttocks washed at about 5.30 p.m. with freshly-aired clothes put on. As the baby gets older, play and kicking times are introduced; at first for, perhaps, about ten minutes before the morning and evening wash, these times being gradually lengthened.

By six months, the baby may be awake and playful for some time in the morning and at lunch-time and again from about 4 p.m. until bath-time, which at this age may be given in the evening rather than the morning. It is usually best to give the baby play and exercise before feeds rather than after them. After bringing up the wind, the baby should be tucked up comfortably in his cot or pram and left to go to sleep. Occasionally he may need lifting to bring up more wind and then be resettled. It is a mistake to start the practice of rocking a baby to sleep as this can become a wearysome chore.

Routine at One Year

At one year a baby may not have an afternoon sleep but he should still have a morning sleep of about 1½-2 hours and this sleep, or rest period, should be maintained even if the baby does not always sleep. As the baby gets older it may be better to have a daytime rest of about one hour after having his lunch at about 12.30 p.m. and such a daily rest should be part of a day's routine throughout early childhood. It is helpful to the mother as well as the toddler, who can have books and toys in bed with him.

Sleep

It is helpful to train the baby to sleep through the night as soon as possible, but in the early weeks the baby may regularly wake at about 2 a.m.-3 a.m. and need a night feed.

Play and Stimulation

Over-stimulating a baby in the early days can result in an over-excited nervous system, but some play is very desirable, and the mother must have the joy of showing off her baby to visitors. Between 4 p.m. and 5.30 p.m. is an excellent time for this.

Sunshine and Fresh Air

Just as a plant needs sunshine and fresh air, so does a baby, and provided the baby is properly clothed, fresh air is very desirable – it is draughts that are undesirable. The pram hood should not be right up or the apron raised except in wet weather. Sunshine and careful sunbathing can be begun from an early age. At first the legs should be exposed to the sun for just one or two minutes, but gradually the time can be lengthened and the amount of skin exposed increased. The eyes and head and back of the neck should be protected with a light sun hat. On no account should the baby's skin become scorched, and in sunny weather it is often best for the baby to be naked in the shade, so that he just benefits from the sun-soaked air, when direct sunlight would be too strong for his delicate skin. It is useful to have a sun canopy for the pram.

Use of a Pot

Opinions differ over potty training. Sir Truby King advocated holding the baby on a small pot after each feed from the earliest days, and motions can sometimes be 'caught' in the pot in this way, but it is hardly a conscious act on the baby's part at first and possibly few mothers may want to carry out this sort of training these busy days, but it can become very effective training for passing both stools and water. Other views are that training can be deferred until the baby is two years old. Two years old seems to be rather late, and most mothers seem to plan to start training in the use of a little pot at about one year, when the baby can begin to understand what is wanted. This training should be done gently and kindly, giving approval when the pot is used but not keeping the baby on it for an extended period, or being cross over wet or soiled napkins when the pot is not used.

Forming Good Habits

The training entailed in a regular routine of meals, sleep, bath and bed and, in due course, his pot, is the baby's first experience of a good behaviour pattern, and such training can be a help to mothers, to have a well organized life.

General Management and Training

The mother's general management should be a matter of love and gentleness in a framework of order and security, and the baby should be accepted as an individual person right from the start. Giving a child too much freedom, though sometimes considered to be very 'modern', can be a cause of considerable unhappiness both for the baby and for his parents if he grows into a tiresome and unmanageable toddler. It is important for the mother to begin as she means to go on, and it is with the wise use of love and approval that the mother can most easily begin to train her baby.

If training in the first year is neglected, the mother may find that she has let slip an invaluable opportunity. A nine-months-old baby can easily learn to understand a firm but kindly 'no', but only if the mother always says 'no' to the same things and always sees that her 'no' is obeyed. There should be as few negatives as possible, but the essential ones must be observed. It is important here that the father says 'no' to the same things in the same way too.

Three or four generations ago some children suffered from excessive training, but now the tendency often seems to be to suffer from a lack of training, so mothers have to reach a happy medium.

Probably the worst thing is a mixture of overtraining and lack of training, which frequently results in the 'spoilt' child. The mother who nags at her child, but does not see that he does what he is told to do, and who may finally give him a good smack, or who has little method or routine for her child, or who lets the child get what he wants by whining or teasing her, is not training at all. Such behaviour by the mother will interfere with her child's happy development and can spoil her own pride and joy in motherhood.

The mother should try to avoid open conflict, and this she can often do with tact, without lessening her own authority. If the child does not want to have his wellington boots on, she can say, 'Which boot shall we put on first?', thus giving the child a choice to think about. It is an essential part of a parents' job to help their baby to be independent, and to be self-reliant and able to stand on his own feet at the appropriate time. Breast-feeding and mothering in the early months are most valuable in giving the baby a sense of well-being and security from which he can, in due course, safely venture out into wider interests.

Smacking

Some people genuinely believe that smacking is an essential part of good nursery training. This, however, is not necessarily true, and where the rudiments of essential training are given in the early months of life, and where approval and encouragement and sometimes rewards are used to get the child to do what is wanted, it should seldom be necessary to smack a child. Smacking can then be discarded as a normal instrument of policy in the nursery. A child who is smacked is being taught to smack, so a smacked child will tend to smack other people. Above all else, the baby needs to have a sense of security and of being loved. He needs to see love in his mother's face and to feel it in her hands, and children are the most loving little creatures in the world, and will forgive our shortcomings over and over again when they feel that they are really much beloved.

Introducing the New Baby to the Toddler

It is important to introduce the new baby wisely to the toddler, if there is one. There should be no mystery about the coming of a new baby, and he can easily understand that a new baby is growing in his mummy's tummy, and that he grew there too. He should understand that the new little brother or sister will be a *baby*, and not yet like himself. It is important that the toddler should never feel that the new baby is taking his mother's love away from him, but from the first should feel that it is 'his' baby too. The mother should see that she has some time every day to devote to the toddler so that he really enjoys the enlargement of his family and does not feel in the slightest degree pushed aside for it. Breast-feeding should also be simply explained.

16.

Minor Troubles of Babies

The mother should aim to prevent any minor upsets. When babies have the right kind of food, particularly breast milk, and receive proper care, they are not very likely to get ill, but some minor upsets may occur, so it is as well to know a bit about them.

If the trouble is severe, or continues, it is always wisest to get expert advice.

Allergies
Sometimes a baby may be sensitive or intolerant to some food which other babies can digest perfectly well, e.g. some babies are sensitive or 'allergic' to cow's milk, which can lead to colds or eczema, or are sensitive to eggs, or they are allergic to the protein of wheat. If there is evidence of an allergic reaction to some food, this is best omitted for the time being, and expert advice sought.

Anaemia
In the first few months of life, the baby draws on a store of iron in his own body, placed there during pregnancy, which is one reason for the importance of the mother having a good diet. Milk contains little iron, so from an early age the baby can have tiny quantities of diluted orange juice to supply iron. This can be started at one or two months and other juices can gradually be introduced.

Sore Buttocks
If the baby's buttocks become red and sore it can be a sign of errors in the diet. Too much sugar or starch or fat, or even too much orange juice may produce sore buttocks, so these foods

should be temporarily reduced and the baby's whole diet reviewed.

Again, if wet or soiled nappies are left on the baby, or if the buttocks are not sponged after removing soiled napkins, the buttocks may also be made sore, so cleanliness and care with the napkins are essential. The napkins are best washed without soda, very well rinsed and dried out of doors if possible. Treatment of sore buttocks apart from reviewing the diet, is to cleanse the affected parts gently with warm water and pat dry very gently, or if severe, cleanse with olive oil. Temporarily, two pieces of old handkerchief, soaked in olive oil can be placed on each buttock to help to prevent the stools from reaching the damaged skin.

Catarrh and Colds

Small babies, either breast-fed or bottle-fed, and who have had a mother who took proper care of herself during her pregnancy, are not at all likely to have a cold if properly fed in the early months, sensibly clothed and given adequate fresh air, but guarded against chills or damp. If a severe cold develops, then the baby may possibly miss a meal, and have just cooled, boiled water, flavoured with fruit juice (such as prune or orange juice) or clear vegetable broth to drink. If the nose becomes blocked, it can generally be cleansed with twists of cotton wool. If there is a rise of temperature, expert advice should be sought.

Circumcision

Sometimes the foreskin of boy babies is a bit tight, and then it may be cut, and this is circumcision. If it is only a little bit tight, the operation may not be necessary, as the foreskin can be gently retracted by the mother each day when the baby is in the bath during the first few weeks of life, and this can be sufficient to cure the tightness and so make the operation unnecessary.

Coeliac Disease

Digestive processes can be disturbed if the baby is allergic to wheat protein, when they have to have a gluten-free diet. Wheat, oats, barley and rye all contain gluten and all have to be cut out of the child's meals. This condition is sometimes thought to be due to the too early introduction of cereals, i.e. before six months.

Colic

Colic is really acute indigestion, and sometimes it can give the baby a lot of pain, and induce a lot of crying, and the mother may think that the baby is hungry, and may give him more food, which he does not need. It can be particularly troublesome in the first three months of life. With breast-fed babies it may be due to the baby getting his milk too quickly, or getting too much of it, or the mother's own diet may need revising. With bottle-fed babies the milk mixture should be carefully checked, and temporarily given slightly more diluted. Care should also be taken to make sure that drinks of diluted fruit juices are not given close to a milk-feed. An opportunity to bring up wind should be given before giving a feed, as well as in the middle of it and at the end.

Constipation

The failure to pass a stool every day is sometimes regarded as constipation, but with breast-fed babies this is not necessarily true. Breast milk may be so good, and so well utilised, that there is little waste to pass, and provided that the stool is normal when passed, i.e. soft and yellow, the mother need not worry at its infrequency, provided that the baby is thriving and gaining weight normally. If not gaining weight adequately and the stools are scanty, then a little longer at the breast may be indicated.

In artificially-fed babies the milk mixture may be a little too strong, and may need reducing. Also, sieved carrots or sieved prunes may be added to the baby's meals, and extra drinks of water or diluted juices may be given. Occasionally constipation may be due to under-feeding, so the baby's weight and weekly gains must also be considered.

Diarrhoea

If the baby has frequent green stools and is not thriving or putting on adequate weight, it is wisest to seek expert advice.

Eczema

Babies sometimes develop extremely painful and irritating eczema, which is one of the most tiresome troubles of babyhood. It is more usual in artificially-fed, than in breast-fed babies, but breast-fed babies may also suffer. If it occurs on the scalp, it may be due to neglected dandruff. It can have a hereditary background, and may be associated with hay fever or asthma, but it seems to be most frequently associated with an allergic reaction to cow's milk, though excess of sugar or the too early introduction of cereal foods or even excess of orange juice can also aggravate the problem.

Rarely is it desirable to wean a breast-fed baby because of eczema, but in such cases the mother should look to her own diet, making sure she is not constipated, and should increase her consumption of vegetables, and vegetable broth. It may help if she herself omits cow's milk and uses Plamil instead, and she should also make sure that she does not have too much sugar. Artificially-fed babies should be taken right off all cow's milk, and substitute a good plant milk, or, if available, they can have goats' milk. Potato water can also be helpful.

For external treatment, the affected parts may be bathed with Epsom salts in water (one teaspoonful to one cupful) and gently patted dry. Some forms of eczema benefit from having a light dressing of olive oil or corn oil put on afterwards. The baby must be kept from scratching the irritating places. Constipation and overweight can aggravate the trouble.

Infectious Diseases

Babies under one year often seem to be immune to infectious diseases, especially if breast-fed, but the baby should stop having milk feeds as soon as he goes off his food or has a temperature, and water or well diluted fruit juices given instead. The doctor's advice should be sought.

Rickets

Rickets is a deficiency disease which should not occur if the feeding is right and if the baby has plenty of sunshine and fresh air. It is usually associated with a diet where there is a deficiency of vitamins A and D and/or an excess of starch.

Sunshine on the skin is an excellent source of vitamin D, but care must be taken not to over-expose the skin to the sun. Cream, butter and egg yolk also supply this vitamin, and the D.H.S.S. supplies vitamin drops especially for babies to supply these vitamins and vitamin C.

Scurf

This sometimes appears on a baby's scalp. The baby's head should be regularly washed each day, gently patted dry, and may then be softly brushed with a soft baby hair brush to keep the scalp in good condition. If scurf, or dandruff, does appear, it should be treated with a piece of cotton wool dipped in warm olive oil and the oil gently applied with a circular motion. It can then be left on all night, and much of the scurf will be removed when the head is washed the next day, but the scalp should not be rubbed to try to remove the scurf. The application of the oil should be repeated until the skin is clear.

Scurvy

Scurvy is a deficiency disease due to a shortage of vitamin C, but it is uncommon in England.

Sickness

See 'Vomiting'.

Stools

The normal stool of a breast-fed baby is soft and yellow, about the colour of made mustard. In artificially-fed babies it may be more formed and of a paler colour.

Small white curds in the stools are usually made of fat, and their presence does not seem to matter unless they are excessive or the baby is ill.

Dark or black stools. The first stools will be dark or black due to the presence of the meconium, but this is normal, and the stools will soon become yellow.

Green stools may be a sign of indigestion, but an occasional green stool is nothing to worry about. If a stool turns green on the napkin later on, it is of less significance. Green stools can occur with both over-feeding and under-feeding.

Pale clay-like stools are usually a sign of a disordered liver.

White, tough, chalky stools are apt to occur if unmodified or insufficiently diluted cow's milk is given to the baby in quantity, when too young.

Hard dry stools are a form of constipation, possibly due to lack of adequate fluid, or other dietetic errors.

Frothy stools are a sign of fermentation, probably due to an excess of sugar or cereal starch.

Abnormal stools should be treated by diet adjustments rather than by medicines, unless these are prescribed by a doctor.

Teething

Ideally the baby should cut his teeth without too much upset. The teeth are growing all the time, but there appear to be periods of 'active teething' when the baby may be fretful and a little off his food. If so, milk feeds may be slightly reduced and extra water and vegetable broth given. The baby should not be persuaded to take milk that he does not want. A bone ring to bite on, (or a piece of baked bread if the gums are not too sore for this) will help the baby's teeth to come through.

Thumb Sucking

Though a little thumb sucking will do no harm, and can be a comfort to a baby, it does not want to develop into such a habit that the baby is always doing it. It is then not good for the baby's teeth, and is an unattractive habit if carried on after babyhood. It may be a sort of compensation for some dissatisfaction, so the mother should see that her baby is correctly fed and has lots of love and caressing through breast-feeding and wise mothering.

Vomiting

If a baby is gaining weight well, but regularly vomits, it is probably being overfed. If it just brings up a little food with its wind, this does not count as vomiting. There is no advantage in feeding a baby until he vomits, as some people used to think. The right amount of food should be estimated and given. Sudden and severe vomiting indicates some trouble and should be dealt with by complete abstinence from milk-feeds and as much water and other fluids given as the baby wants to have. Vomiting and failure to gain weight needs expert advice.

Weight and Weighing
The baby's weight is a good general guide to his progress, and at first he should be weighed each week to check his progress, at a weekly baby clinic. If all is going well, after weekly weighings for about six weeks, the weighings may be done every fortnight.

Wind
When sucking either breast or bottle the baby may swallow some air with the milk. He should be held up against the mother's shoulder halfway through a feed and again at the end, having his back gently rubbed upwards to help him to bring up the wind. Until he has done this, he may not feed so well and is unlikely to settle to sleep properly, and may cry soon after he is put into his cot. Even if he has brought up some wind he may need to be picked up again, and again helped to bring up a little more wind.

17.

Minor Troubles of Expectant and Nursing Mothers

While having a baby is a perfectly natural process, sometimes difficulties may arise. To help mothers prepare for possible trials and to deal with them satisfactorily, a brief account of some of them is included here. Following the earlier instructions given in this book should help to minimize potential troubles.

After Pains
These are cramp-like pains that occur perhaps for a few days after the birth. They are the result of the contractions of the uterus, and gentle exercise and deep breathing will help the essential contracting process. They are generally strongest when the baby starts to suck, but breast-feeding helps the proper contraction of the uterus and the severity of the contractions soon decreases.

Backache
If this is severe it indicates the need for extra rest, and lying on the front can help, also the use of a high stool for carrying out as many jobs as possible.

Breast Engorged
In the first week or two after the baby is born, the breasts are very active and may sometimes become very full and painful. This is called 'engorgement' and there may have been some degree of overfeeding or too much fluid may have been taken.

The breasts may become so full that the baby has difficulty in getting hold of the nipple, but as he should already have learnt to suckle, before the breasts got hard, he will persevere, though it may be a bit painful for the mother. Relief comes as the baby draws off some of the milk. Between feeds the breasts should be firmly and comfortably supported, and if necessary, a *little* of the excess milk may be drawn off with a breast pump, but much milk should not be drawn off or the breasts will just be stimulated to secrete more. The mother should reduce her fluids a little, just temporarily for a day or two, and check over her diet, and be sure to avoid any degree of constipation.

Constipation

It is essential to avoid any tendency to constipation during pregnancy and breast-feeding, and the diet suggested here, particularly 100 per cent wholewheat bread, exercise, deep breathing, fresh air and adequate fluids, including vegetable broth, will in many cases prevent it occurring. If it does materialize, purgatives should not be used, but fruits and vegetables may be increased, and extra unprocessed bran taken with muesli for breakfast (two or more teaspoonsful as needed to secure a daily, easy, soft motion).

Figure

The breasts should be comfortably supported during pregnancy and breast-feeding, and exercises for the arms and neck and shoulders are helpful in keeping the breasts firm. Also exercises to strengthen the abdomen should be done regularly to help the mother to regain her natural figure.

Greedy Appetite

Occasionally a mother may find that she has developed an enormous appetite, generally for the less desirable items of food, and yet she always seems hungry. A good appetite is healthy, but overeating may lead to many troubles. If her appetite is for fruit, this is different, as it is hardly possible to eat too much fruit, especially if eaten by itself. Apart from fruit, the mother should normally have just three meals a day, and should not have 'nibbles' of cakes, biscuits or sweets between them.

A perpetual 'hungry feeling' is really a form of indigestion, and can be helped with a glass of hot lemonade or other diluted fruit or vegetable drink, but she may also need to exercise strong will power and determination not to eat too much. It will help her to keep away from the sight or smell of food, and to ease the urge she can also very slowly chew a few raisins or suck a prune.

Miscarriage

Occasionally the developing embryo may become detached from the wall of the uterus and discharged from the body. The times when it is most liable to happen are the first day or two when a period would have occurred, especially in the third month, so a little extra care at these times is only sensible. Abdominal pains and signs of bleeding would be a warning of a possible miscarriage, and if these occur the mother should at once go to bed. She should also consult her doctor. Shocks, accidents such as a fall, straining at some job, or extreme emotion can bring on a miscarriage. Occasionally, it may be due to nature getting rid of a damaged foetus, in which case a miscarriage would be a blessing in disguise.

A miscarriage is a weakening and depressing event, but the mother, though sad, should not let herself brood over it, but should concentrate, with her husband's help, on getting herself fit and well again so that she can look forward to having another baby in the future.

Morning Sickness

(See Chapter 4.)

Nipples

In a healthy, well-fed mother, the skin of the nipples is soft and elastic and able to take the baby's sucking without cracking. They should be patted dry after each feed and washed night and morning. Should a crack appear it should be kept scrupulously clean and dry and it may be wisest to use a nipple shield for feeding until the crack heels. Lanolin or Friar's Balsam can be applied to the nipple after feeding and cleansing, but should be washed off before the next feed.

Tiredness

It is not surprising for the mother to feel a little extra tired when carrying or feeding her baby, even if things are going well. She should regard it as a demand on the part of her body for some extra rest, either a lying down rest after her midday meal, or going to bed earlier. She should not drive herself to go on when feeling tired or she may sap her own and her baby's vitality. There may be some errors in her diet, so this should be checked over, a daily supplement such as Bemax (wheatgerm) for B and E vitamins may be a good plan or perhaps a tablet of kelp (seaweed) or a tablet of bone-meal for natural mineral salts.

Varicose Veins

These should not normally occur if the mother has the right kind of food, fresh air and exercise, but she should avoid unnecessary standing about, doing such housework as she can sitting down or on a high stool, and should have the foot of her bed raised two to three inches on small blocks of wood. A brisk walk is generally helpful, and it is best to have expert advice.

18.

Recipes

Bread – 100 Per Cent Wholewheat

$1\frac{1}{2}$ lb (675g) 100 per cent wholewheat stone-ground flour (if possible organically grown)
$1\frac{1}{2}$ teaspoonsful salt (sea salt if available)
$\frac{1}{2}$ oz (15g) dried yeast (3 level teaspoonsful) or 1 oz (25g) fresh yeast
1 teaspoonful muscavado sugar
$\frac{3}{4}$ pint (850ml) and 2 tablespoonsful lukewarm water

Add sugar to two tablespoonsful of lukewarm water, sprinkle on the dried yeast, whisk and leave to stand in a warm (not hot) place for about ten minutes, after which time the surface should be covered with a thick layer of bubbles. If using fresh yeast also mix with the sugar and water, but it may not take quite so long to work.

Put flour and salt in a mixing bowl to warm. Make a well in the centre of the flour, stir up the worked yeast and pour into the flour, and add $1\frac{1}{2}$ pints (850ml) of the lukewarm water. Work all well together to make a soft even lump of dough. As a rough guide it should be softer than pastry but not as soft as a fruit cake.

Turn out onto a well-floured board and knead strongly for five to ten minutes, turning the dough round to get a fresh edge to turn into the centre, and pressing down hard with the knuckles. Put back into the bowl, cover with a damp cloth and leave in a warm (not hot) place to prove for about 35 minutes. A warm kitchen, or the airing cupboard, or standing in a bowl of warm water will do.

The dough will now have considerably increased in size, and be soft and spongy. Turn it out onto a floured board and knead again lightly. Have ready two warmed and greased one-pound bread tins and a baking tray. Take two pieces of the dough each of 1 lb (450g), knead to the shape of the tins, put the dough into the tins, cover with a damp cloth and leave to rise again in a warm place until about ½ inch (1¼cm) above the edge of the tins. Make the rest of the dough into a batch of rolls and put them on the baking tray to rise also.

When risen, put the loaves into a hot oven, pre-heated to 450°F/230°C (Gas Mark 8), and bake until the loaves are light golden brown, and sound 'done' when tapped (in about 35-40 minutes). Turn out onto wire rack to cool. The rolls take a shorter cooking time.

Baked Bread

Cut a couple of fairly thick slices of 100 per cent wholewheat bread into fingers and leave in a cool oven until crisp, hard and golden brown. Useful for babies to chew at, or may be eaten with butter and honey or a savoury spread.

Boiled Eggs for Babies

Boiling eggs makes the white rather tough, so for babies a saucepan containing enough water to well cover an egg should be brought to the boil and the egg put in, the lid put on and the pan removed from the heat. After seven to ten minutes the egg will be cooked with the white firm, but neither jellyish nor tough.

Brose

  1 tablespoonful medium oatmeal
  1 teaspoonful sea salt
  1 pint (575ml) boiling water
  Some fresh fruit or fresh fruit juice (optional)

Put salt and oatmeal in a jug and pour on the boiling water, stir and leave to draw and get cold. Strain and drink hot or cold. A most refreshing drink when tired. Cleaned orange or apple peelings, or something such as blackcurrant for flavouring, may be added. Dr A.B. Cunning strongly recommends it for ailing or difficult children.

Carrot Juice

A fresh, good carrot.

Scrub carrot very thoroughly, cutting out any damaged parts. It is best not to scrape it. If to be used for babies, dip a carrot into boiling water just for a second to sterilize it. Grate the carrot using a two-way grater onto a piece of butter muslin freshly wrung out of boiling water and placed in a dish. Fold the sides of the muslin over the grated carrot and twist the ends as though for a poultice, and the juice will run out, and should be drunk at once. The amount of juice does vary according to the carrots.

Cole Slaw

1 tablespoonful chopped celery (strings first removed)
1 tablespoonful chopped brussels sprouts
1 tablespoonful grated raw carrots
A few seedless raisins
Salad cream

Combine well together in home-made salad cream, and serve with one or two pieces of tomato, watercress, lettuce or home-grown cress or mustard.

Conservatively Cooked Vegetables

To cook vegetables conservatively, they should be cooked in a minimum of water for the shortest time needed to make them tender, and any water left should be used as a drink or for making sauces, etc. The vegetables after being washed and any damaged parts removed, should be cut up small and put in either a saucepan with a little water and the lid on, or in a dish in the oven with a little water and the lid on. Care must be taken to see that they do not burn, and a little more water may need to be added as the cooking proceeds. Just a minimum of sea salt may be added, but no soda. This method of cooking is carried out to conserve the mineral salts and as far as possible the vitamins of the vegetables.

Gentian Root Tea*

Gentian root
Boiling water

* Consult your doctor before taking this herb.

Put one large tablespoonful of gentian root (obtainable from herbalists) into a jug, and pour on one pint (575ml) of boiling water. Stir, cover and leave to draw. A teacupful either cold or reheated may be drunk two or three times a day when nausea is troublesome.

Gravy

Thicken some vegetable broth and flavour with Marmite.

Honey Tea

¼ cupful creamy milk
¾ cupful hot water
1 teaspoonful honey

Combine and drink as desired.

Muesli (Home-made)

3 tablespoonsful rolled oats
1 tablespoonful each of Bemax, powdered dried milk, unprocessed bran and ground almonds

Mix these all together and keep in a covered jar. Serve two or three tablespoonsful of the muesli with a chopped-up eating apple and one dessertspoonful of seedless raisins and some milk, as a main breakfast dish. Two or three times this amount can be prepared at a time to save trouble. Other fruits can be used for variety, and soaked and simmered prunes or apricots also make a delicious muesli.

Rusks (savoury)

4 slices of wholewheat bread (about ½ inch thick)
2 tablespoonsful vegetable broth
1 dessertspoonful Marmite or Barmene

Cut the bread into fingers. Dissolve Marmite in the vegetable broth. Put the fingers of bread into the Marmite solution turning them over to make sure that they are wet all over. Drain off excess fluid and put on a greased baking tin and leave in a warm oven until crisp and light brown.

Rusks (sweet)

Proceed as above, but use one dessertspoonful honey in two tablespoonsful of water instead of the Marmite solution.

Savoury Celery Sticks

Celery
Cream cheese
Parsley
Watercress

Wash and string some celery sticks, and cut into two-inch lengths. Fill with cream cheese and sprinkle with a little chopped parsley or other herbs, and allow four sticks per person. Serve on watercress.

Salad

1 or 2 root vegetables
1 or 2 leaf vegetables
1 or 2 fruits or flowers
Dressing of oil and lemon juice or yogurt or home-made salad cream

Wash and clean the vegetables, and cut up or grate them as liked and arrange attractively on individual plates. It is a good plan to use a different variety of vegetables during the week. Chopped brussels sprouts are excellent in the winter months, and a slice of avocado pear is very nice when not too expensive.

Toast Sandwich

Slice of fairly thick wholewheat bread, toasted
Fillings as desired

Slit the toast while still hot, and leave to cool. Then spread cut sides with butter, and spread one side with the chosen filling, such as minced dates, banana and honey, cream cheese with well-chopped lettuce or watercress, etc. Put the other half of the toast on top of the filling and press firmly together. May be cut into little squares for babies to feed themselves with after about eight months.

Vegetable Broth

Cleaned outer leaves of finely chopped celery stalks, leeks, pea pods, etc. may be added when making vegetable broth, and vegetable broth is an excellent use for old runner beans. As well as using the outer parts, add finely chopped-up carrots and onions and some parsley to make two pounds (900g) of well-chopped vegetables. Add four pints (2.3 litres) of water and one *bouquet garni* sachet and simmer for 45 minutes. Strain and add a taste of sea salt and a taste of Marmite if liked.

It is an excellent drink for expectant mothers and nursing mothers. It may be taken half-and-half with milk, hot or cold.

Vegetable and Lentil Soup

4 oz (100g) each of onions, carrots, celery and tomatoes
6 oz (175g) lentils
Bouquet garni
Sea salt
2 pints (1 litre, approx.) vegetable broth or water or stock

Wash the lentils and put into enough water, salted with sea salt, to cover them, bring to the boil, and boil gently until tender, stirring to prevent sticking, adding more water if necessary. Cut the vegetables up small and put into two pints (about one litre) boiling vegetable water with the *bouquet garni* and salt and cook until tender. Sieve the cooked lentils and add them and any broth left to the cooked vegetables and season to taste.

If liked the whole soup may be sieved, and this may be well liked if morning sickness is present, or a few teaspoonsful can be given to babies as one of their 'extras'.

Herbs

Herbs can be used chopped up in salads or as flavours in savoury dishes, according to individual tastes, as can also garlic, but some people do not like garlic very much, so it should only be used with discretion.

Appendix I

Teeth and Fluoridation

Good teeth are very important and they should be created through the eating of high quality food, beginning in the mother's pregnancy, and continuing through childhood and adolescence, and by avoiding, as far as possible, white sugar in all its tempting forms, and white flour.

Fluoridation is an attempt to reduce dental decay among children by adding a fluoride at the rate of one part per million to the public's drinking water, but this is a most undesirable procedure.

Firstly, because it is quite unethical to compel everyone to take a daily dose of fluoride, often against their will, by putting it into the public drinking water.

Secondly, it has not been proved to be absolutely safe, and no-one could guarantee that fifty million people could drink artificially fluoridated water for fifty years with neither them nor their children suffering any harm from doing so. Among other evidence of harm, Dr Waldbott, in America, has shown that some people may be allergic to fluoridated water.

Thirdly, the alleged benefits of fluoridation are much less than is claimed. The Ministry of Health's own 'Report on Eleven Years of Fluoridation' shows that, at the age of eight, children who have always drunk fluoridated water have about one fewer decayed tooth than do children who have not drunk fluoridated water, but that after this age the rate of increase in decay is about the same with, or without the fluoride.

Dental decay is not due to a shortage of fluoride, but to an excess of sugar and white flour. Unfortunately, fluoridation of our drinking water is a convenient way of getting rid of waste industrial fluorides.

Expectant mothers should not take fluoride tablets. The

body gets all the fluoride that it needs in natural forms in minute traces in various natural unrefined foods, such as 100 per cent wholewheat bread.

Appendix II

Sterility

It can be a great grief to some women when they want a baby and conception does not take place, and there are fertility clinics where such parents can go for help and advice. Even before going to such a clinic, such parents would be wise to adopt some helpful measures themselves. They should adopt a whole, natural diet, with plenty of B vitamins (taking Bemax or Froment) and 100 per cent wholewheat bread and some vitamin E capsules, and kelp tablets for mineral salts, and no white sugar or white bread or white flour product and plenty of salads and fruits. They should not smoke at all. The mother should also try not to keep on thinking about having a baby, but should try to be relaxed and happy in her daily life, doing interesting and enjoyable things with her husband.

Appendix III

Contraceptive Pill

If a woman has been taking the contraceptive pill, she would be wise to take a complete vitamin B supplement for a short time before starting a pregnancy.

Appendix IV

Friction Rub

To stimulate the activity of the skin and improve its health, the friction rub is very helpful. There are various ways of carrying this out, and it may be done wet or dry. If done wet, there should be a quick dry rub with a rough towel to finish it off. It may be done with:

1. A soft brush.
2. A pair of loofah gloves.
3. A rough wet or dry towel.

The mother, with no clothes on, should systematically brush or rub her whole body, covering every inch of her skin as far as she can. Using a pair of loofah gloves is probably the best way of doing this. In the main she should work from the extremities towards the heart, and the rub should take several minutes. The wet rub is said to be more effective, but if it seems a little chilly, the dry one can be used to good effect.

Glossary of Some Food Supplements

Acerola. Natural vitamin C tablets.

Apple Juice. Pure, unfermented bottled apple juice, available in bottles or cartons. It is an excellent drink, either plain or diluted.

Baby Familia. Baby muesli, specially prepared for babies. Can be introduced in small amounts from about six months.

Barmene. Savoury spread similar to Marmite, containing vitamin B_{12}

Bemax. A natural wheatgerm rich in the vitamin B group, vitamin E, protein, iron, manganese and copper. Alternative: Froment.

Bickie Pegs. Hard little fingers for the baby to chew at.

Bone Meal. Mineral salts supplement. Recommended by Dr Aslander for building good teeth.

Bran Plus. Outer coats of wheat, with the wheatgerm. An excellent source of fibre and invaluable for treating constipation.

Brewer's Yeast. Provides B vitamins.

Froment. Natural wheatgerm, rich in vitamin B group, vitamin E, protein, iron, manganese and copper. Alternative: Bemax.

Gentian Root Tea.* A herbal infusion made from the dried gentian roots. Helpful for allaying morning sickness (obtainable from herbalists).

Haliborange. A vitamin preparation, rich in vitamins A, C and D, prepared from halibut oil and orange juice.

Kelp. Seaweed, a source of mineral salts.

Molasses. A useful source of iron. May be taken on bread or in water as a drink, or in capsules.

* Consult your doctor before taking this herb.

Plamil. Milk of plant origin used as an alternative to cow's milk. Generally obtainable from health food stores. Useful in cases of an allergy to cow's milk.

Raspberry Leaf Tea. Obtainable from herbalists. Excellent traditional drink for pregnancy and the confinement.

Soya Flour. A valuable vegetarian protein food, made from the soya bean, rich also in mineral salts and vitamins A, B and D. May be served with fruit or made into savoury sauces or to enrich cakes (obtainable from health food stores).

Yeastrel. Similar to Marmite.

Useful Addresses

The National Childbirth Trust, 9 Queensborough Terrace, London W2.

The Birth Centre, 16 Simpson Street, London SW2.

Foresight, Woodhurst, Hydestyle, Godalming, Surrey.

Winganna Natural Fleeces, Sandyhill Enterprises, 9 Brookside, St Ishmaels, Haverfordwest, Dyfed SA62 3TE.

Vita Florum Products, Cats Castle, Lydeard St Lawrence, Taunton, Somerset TA4 3QA.

Mothercare, P.O. Box 145, Watford, Herts WD2 5SH.

Soil Association, Walnut Tree Manor, Haughley, Stowmarket, Suffolk.

Society to Support Home Confinements, Mrs M. Whyte, 17 Laburnum Avenue, Durham City, Durham.

Further Reading

Balfour, Lady Eve: *The Living Soil*, Faber.

Barfield, Mary: *Relaxation for Childbirth*, Fontana.

Brook, Danae: *Nature Birth*, Spearman.

Heardman, Helen: *A Way to Natural Childbirth*, Churchill Livingston.

Grant, Doris: *Your Daily Food: Your Recipe for Survival*, Faber.

Haire, Doris: *The Cultural Warping of Childbirth*, International Childbirth Education Association.

Hills, Hilda Cherry: *Good Food Gluten Free*, Henry Doubleday Research Association.

Leboyer, Dr Frederick: *Birth Without Violence*, Fontana.

Lief, Stanley: *How to Eat for Health*, Thorsons.

Mackarness, Dr Richard: *Not All in the Mind*, Pan Books.

Read, Dr Grantly Dick: *Childbirth Without Fear*, Pan Books.

Stanway, Drs Penny and Andrew: *Breast is Best*, Pan Books.

Vellay, Dr Pierre: *Childbirth Without Pain*, Hutchinson.

Index

Index